F.H. Hoadley

Human Discords

F.H. Hoadley

Human Discords

ISBN/EAN: 9783337370190

Printed in Europe, USA, Canada, Australia, Japan

Cover: Foto ©Thomas Meinert / pixelio.de

More available books at **www.hansebooks.com**

HUMAN DISCORDS

A

STUDY IN MEDICAL PSYCHOLOGY
WITH DESCRIPTIVE CASES
COLLECTED BY
F. H. H.

Published for Private Distribution

HUMAN DISCORDS

SIR THOMAS BROWNE, in his *Religio Medici*, says : "It is my temper, and I like it the better, to affect all harmony. * * * for there is music wherever there is harmony, order or proportion; and thus far we maintain the *music of the spheres;* for these well ordered motions and regular paces, though they give no sound to the ear, yet to the understanding they strike a note most full of harmony. * * * It is the hieroglyphical and shadowed lesson of the whole world, and creatures of God ; such a melody to the ear, as the whole world well understood, would afford the understanding."

> Was ich *soll?* Wer löst mir je die Frage ?
> Was ich *kann ?* Wer gönnt mir den Versuch ?
> Was ich *muss?* Vermag' ich's ohne Klage ?
> So viel Arbeit für ein Leichentuch !—PLATEN.

"It is only with renunciation that life, properly speaking, can be said to begin."—GOETHE.

HUMAN DISCORDS.

The meditations of the philosopher cannot be uninfluenced, nor the heart of the philanthropist unmoved, by the facts, which statistics prove, that there are, at the present moment, in the United States alone, more than 106,000 people who are deprived of all their active rights as human beings, and made, as far as possible, nonentities in the world.* About 52,000 of these are actually shut up in lunatic asylums, and of that number but very few are ever likely to leave their undesired abode, until they take their leave of life itself. It cannot therefore be unprofitable to endeavor, in one department of an extensive subject, to follow the course of mental degeneration, and by the exhibition of it, to justify the world's treatment of the particular discords in nature's general harmony.

It is a well known fact that, from an early period of speculative thought, two doctrines have been held with regard to the sort of connection which exists between a man's mind and his body.

On the one hand there are those who maintain that mind is an outcome and function of matter, in a certain state of organization, coming with it, growing with it, decaying with it, inseparable from it. On the other hand there are those who hold that mind is an independent spiritual essence, which has entered into the body, as its dwelling place for a time, which makes use of it as its mortal instrument, and which will take

---

* It must always be borne in mind that under "Insane" the American Census does not include idiots. If these be added the proportion to the population would be raised from about 1 in 560 to 1 in 300.

on its independent life when the body, worn out by the operation of natural decay, returns to the earth of which it is made.

Without entering into a discussion as to which is the true doctrine, it will be sufficient for our purpose to accept and proceed from the generally admitted fact that all the manifestations of mind, which we have to do with in this world, are connected with organization, dependent upon it, whether as cause or instrument; that they are never met with apart from it any more than electricity, or any other natural force, is met with apart from matter, and that higher organization must go along with higher mental function. What is the state of things in another world—whether the disembodied or celestially embodied spirits of the countless myriads of the human race that have come and gone through countless ages are now living higher lives—I do not venture to inquire. One hope and one certitude in the matter everyone may be allowed to have and to express; the hope that, if they are living now, it is a higher life than they lived upon earth; the certitude that, if they are living a higher life, most of them must have had a vast deal to unlearn.

Many persons, who admit, in general terms, the dependence of mental function on cerebral structure, are inclined, when brought to the particular test, to make an exception in favor of moral feeling, or conscience. Some popular capital has been made and made in quarters, where we might justly have looked for greater sincerity and sounder apprehension, out of the fact that physiology, however far it may advance, can never bridge over the gap between nerve element and mind, can never leap from the movements of molecules to consciousness. No one has ever said that it could. The problem before us as scientific observers is not to demonstrate the real nature of the force which we designate as mental, nor to show how and why certain molecular movements in nerve become, if they do become, sensation or idea, but it is to trace here, as in other departments of nature, uniformities of sequence, to point out that certain sequences are, within our experience, the invariable consequences of certain antecedent conditions. The *how* or the *why* is a mystery which we do not attempt to explain ; we do not even aspire to know it. What is the actual power, which makes one body attract another directly as the mass, and inversely as the square of the distance, we have not the least knowledge ; why and how certain molecular movements become heat, light, electricity, or chemical action, we are just as ignorant ; in offering no explanation of the *why* certain states of matter occasion certain states of mind, we acknowledge a mystery neither more nor less in the one case than in the other. To say that it is inconceivable that matter, in however complicated a state of organization, should feel and think, is simply to appeal to the self sufficiency of the human intellect at the present day, and a sort of argument which, if logically carried through would bar any new conception of what, through ignorance, is yet inconceivable to us. It would make the present limit of conception the limit of conception forever ; and it is certainly unwarrantable in the face of the fact that the history of the progress of knowledge is, in great part, the history of the inconceivable becoming conceivable.

There are still many who are content to rest in the same uncertain position which satisfied the well known author of "Inquiries concerning the Intellectual Powers;" who, having pointed out plainly the dependence of mental function on organization, and, as a matter of fact which cannot be denied, that there are individuals in whom every correct feeling in regard to moral relations is obliterated, while the judgment is unimpaired in all other relations, stopped there without attempting to prosecute inquiry into the cause of the remarkable fact which he justly emphasized; and he said, it is "a point in the moral constitution of man which does not belong to the physician to investigate ; the fact is unquestionable ; the solution is to be sought in the records of eternal truth." *

So far from assenting to such an exclusion the physician holds that there is no Holy of Holies in science; he asserts that it distinctly belongs to him to seek for the solution of the problem in the discovery of those laws of nature which are to him the incontestable records of eternal truth.

Whether there is the same essential connection between moral sense and brain, or between any of our special senses and its special ganglionic center in the brain, whether, in short, conscience is a function of organization, is a problem which the medical psychologist, whose duty brings him into constant intercourse with facts, must face; he cannot rest satisfied with vague speculation; he is bound to investigate the phenomena as they present themselves to observation, and to form conclusions from them, without regard to accepted theories of faith or knowledge; if he arrives at sound conclusions, from such observations of facts not before observed, these will not contradict old faiths unless in

---

* Abercrombie, *On the Intellectual Powers.*

that wherein old faiths are wrong and it is right they should be contradicted. His generalizations, like the generalizations of astronomy, or chemistry, or any other branch of science, must rest on their own merits; they cannot justly be tested by any preconceived standard of truth, however much hallowed by antiquity or sanctioned by authority.

So far as the phenomena of deranged mind reach, the battle has been won and the victory is complete. No one, whose opinion is of any value, pretends now that they are anything more than the deranged functions of the supreme nerve centers of the body; but the victory is not yet complete along the whole line of mental function. There is the strongest desire evinced, and the most strenuous efforts are made in many quarters to exempt from physical research the highest functions of mind, and particularly the so-called moral sense and the will. The moral sense is the stronghold of those who have made strategical movements of retreat from other defensive positions they have taken up; and it is from this stronghold that what are deemed the most telling arguments against the Darwinian doctrine of physiological evolution have come.

The observation which makes plain the fact "that this power should so lose its sway while reason remains unimpaired"* does not, however, leave us entirely without information concerning the cause of it, when we pursue it faithfully, since it reveals as distinct a dependence of moral faculty upon organization as of any other faculty.

What is commonly called unconsciousness, or insen-

---

* Abercrombie, *On the Intellectual Powers.*

sibility, is of course one of the most invariable and characteristic of the immediate consequences of all serious injuries of the brain. This state is as a general rule of comparative brief duration, and eventuates either in restoration of consciousness or in its obliteration in death. Sometimes the unconsciousness arising out of injury to the brain is rapid and complete ; in the course of a few minutes the mind is again operating as if nothing had happened. Sometimes recovery is tardy, unconsciousness being maintained for hours, or days, and being gradually replaced by unimpaired mental activity. Rarely the restoration to consciousness is indefinitely postponed, a state resembling deep slumber being continued for weeks or even months or years. Many instructive examples of the pervading mental effects of physical injury of the brain are to be found in medical literature and might be quoted, but a few, well authenticated, will suffice.

In October, 1842, an American medical man, Dr. P. R. Hoy, was called to see a youth, aged eighteen, a resident of New Haven, Ohio, who had been struck down insensible by the kick of a horse. There was a depressed fracture of the skull a little above the left temple. The skull was trephined and the loose fragments of bone that pressed upon the brain were removed, whereupon the patient came to his senses. On the morning of the third day the patient was again unconscious. The wound was opened and a clot of blood together with a small quantity of serum was permitted to escape ; as soon as this cause of pressure was removed the boy became not only conscious but was able to converse freely. The dura was uninjured and the doctor thought it a good opportunity to make an experiment. He asked the boy a question which involved a considerable degree of mental effort and observed that there was immediately a decided increase in the flow of blood in the small vessels of the brain accompanied by an increased motion of the organ, and that the congestion and motion subsided gradually as soon as the mind came to rest. He next asked the boy a question, and, before there was time to answer it, he pressed firmly with his finger upon the exposed brain. As long as the pressure was kept up the boy was mute, but the instant it was removed he made a reply never suspecting that he had not answered at once. This experiment was repeated several times with precisely the same result, the boy's thoughts being stopped and started again, on each occasion, as easily and as certainly as the engineer stops and starts his locomotive.

In August, 1856, an English groom, aged 19, working in Mount Pleasant, Racine County, Wisconsin, was ordered to take the mare, Dolly, to town and leave her colt in the stable. While struggling with the colt the mare kicked the boy on the head. Those who witnessed the accident believed him to be killed, but, seeing that he soon began to breath, sent for a surgeon, Dr. Hoy, who found a fracture with depression at the upper part of the boy's forehead a little to the left of the median line. As soon as the depressed portion of the bone was removed the patient called out, with great energy, "Whoa, Dolly!" and then stared about him in blank amazement, demanding, "Where is the mare? Where am I, what has happened?" Three hours had passed since the accident during which the words which he was just going to utter, when it happened, had remained locked up, as they might have been locked up in a phonograph, to be let go the moment the obstructing pressure was removed. The patient did not remember when he came to himself that the mare had kicked him ; the last thing, before he was insensible, that he did remember was that she wheeled her heels round and laid back her ears viciously.*

I am indebted also to Dr. Hoy for the following remarkable case related by Prof. R. D. Mussy, of the Ohio Medical School, at Cincinnati, to the class of 1840, in a lecture on the physiology of the brain. A man living in Vermont was standing near his mill, bantering with his son about shooting a kingfisher that was perched on a dry snag which projected from the water of the pond. The son fired, and the rifle ball, a small one, missed the bird, ricochetted and struck his father near the middle of the forehead. The man dropped instantly ; he was carried home, and, despite the hopelessness of his recovery, he continued to live on, "a mere animal," incapable of speech, for fifteen years ; about this time a slight elevation of the skull at the crown of the head was discovered. Dr. Mussy, who related the case, trephined the skull at this point ; he found and removed the flattened bullet that had remained so long a time within the skull. Presently the patient called out, "Zeke, you dog, you missed it !" "Missed what ?" asked the doctor. "Why, the kingfisher." This was the first word spoken since the accident, and the old man could not understand that the report of the rifle was not reverberating, at that moment, across the water of the pond.

A lady, whose case is given by Dr. Abercrombie, was seized by an apoplectic attack while engaged at

---

* Journal of Nervous and Mental Diseases, April, 1877.

cards.   The seizure took place on Thursday evening ;
she was in a state of stupor during Friday and Saturday,
and recovered her consciousness rather suddenly on Sun-
day.   The first words she then uttered were, " What is
trump ? "

It is told of a British Captain that at the battle of
the Nile he was giving an order from the quarter deck
of his vessel when a shot struck him on the head depriv-
ing him immediately of speech.   As he survived the injury he was taken home, and remained insensible in
Greenwich Hospital for fifteen months.   At the end of
that period, during which he is said to have manifested
no sign of intelligence, an operation was performed on
his head, which almost instantly restored him to consciousness.   He then immediately arose from his bed
and, not recognizing where he was, or what had occurred, expressed a desire to complete the order which
had been abruptly interrupted when he received the injury fifteen months before.*

A sailor who was wounded in the head while taking
a prize in the Mediterranean in June, 1799, lived, to use
the words of Sir Astley Cooper, " a year unconscious of
his existence."   Mr. Cline, the surgeon, performed on
him the operation of trepanning a year after the injury.
The portion of bone which had been driven in was removed and thus the patient recovered perfectly in a few
days the use of his brain and mental faculties.†

Cases of this kind show how entirely dependent
every function of mind is upon a sound mechanism of
the brain.   Just as we can by pressing upon the sensory
nerve of the arm prevent an impression made upon the

---

* West Riding Reports, 1872.   Vol. II, p. 118.

† West Riding Reports, 1872.   Vol. II. p. 117.

finger being carried to the brain and felt there, so by pressing upon the brain we can as certainly stop a thought or a volition.   In all these cases a good recovery presently followed the removal of the pressure upon the brain; but it would be of no little medical interest to have the after histories of the persons, since it happens sometimes after a serious injury to the head, that despite an immediate recovery, slow degenerative changes are set up in the brain, months or years afterwards, which go on to cause a gradual weakening, and perhaps eventual destruction of mind.

Now the instructive matter in these cases is that the moral character is usually impaired first and sometimes is completely perverted without a corresponding deterioration of the understanding; the person is a thoroughly changed character for the worse.   The injury has produced disorder in the most delicate part of the mental organization, that which is separated from actual contact with the skull only by the thin investing membranes of the brain ; and once damaged it is seldom that it is ever completely restored to its former state of soundness. However, happy recoveries are now and then made from mental derangement caused by physical injury to the brain.

A joiner, who had led a steady life, while at work, and in his usual health, was struck on his head by a hammer that fell from a height of about six feet.   He was not unsensed, nor did any serious symptoms show themselves at the time of the accident ; but afterwards he felt the effects of the blow.   In six months time he began to complain of giddiness ; he gradually lost his power of application and concentration ; he tried to work but had no idea of what he had to do, and could not fix his mind on anything. In the course of a twelve month his symptoms became aggravated ; he grew irritable, morose, violent, and threatened suicide ; he was taken to a hospital where he made a most determined attempt on his life, by throwing himself over from the staircase at the top of the hospital. His life was saved by the courage of one of the nurses, Miss Stockburn, a probationer ; next day, nineteen months after he received the injury, he was taken to an asylum. There was a slight depression at the seat of the injury on the left parietal ; a portion of the skull was removed by the trephine ; no fracture was found and the membranes beneath were apparently healthy. The wound healed rapidly and well ; a decided improvement in nervons symptoms followed. One month after the operation he was lively, and cheerful, and went to work in the carpenter shop. Dr. Bacon, Medical Superintendent of the asylum says : " He steadily improved and was discharged on trial six months after his admission to the asylum ; he went back to his old employers, is still at work, and is reported to be entirely well and fit to be at large."*

A machinist, while working in a foundry, was struck on the top of the head by a stove lifter. He was taken home unconscious and so remained for six hours, and confined to his bed for several days. He was soon able to resume his work which he continued to do for six months. From that time on he became negligent and careless about his clothing, with lack of interest in anything ; finally melancholy and suicidal, and was brought to an asylum, three years after the injury. There was a slight depression of the skull at the point where the blow was received ; the surrounding bone was

* Journal of Mental Science, Jan'y, 1881. Vol. 26, p. 551.

removed by means of a chisel when a spicule of bone the size and shape of a headless carpet tack was found puncturing the dura; this was removed; a water dressing was applied to the wound which healed promptly by direct union. The patient was about on the third day and went home on the seventh day "a new man," as he expressed it, and has been able to continue his work as a stove moulder from that time. Dr. Fletcher, Superintendent of the Indiana State Hospital for the Insane, who reported the case, says: " It is now two years since the man was discharged; he has been perfectly well and has worked at his trade constantly."*

A particularly instructive case was reported by Dr. Holland Skae, Medical Superintendent of the Ayr District Asylum:

Some years ago a young man, no member of his family known to have been insane before, while working in a coal pit, was felled to the ground by a large mass of falling coal, which struck him on the head a little above the left extremity of the left eyelid, causing fracture of the skull at that point. He lay insensible for four days after the accident, when he gradually recovered consciousness, and a few weeks afterwards resumed work in the pit. Not many weeks after doing so, however, his wife and friends began to observe an alteration in his habits and nature which became more and more marked and obtrusive as time progressed. He had formerly been a very cheerful, rather merry, sociable, and good-natured man—what his fellow-workers would have called a "neighbourly chiel"—and at all times previous to the accident was kind and lovable to his wife and children, with whom

---

* American Journal of Insanity, October, 1887, Vol. 44, p. 212.

he delighted to pass his evenings in sober enjoyment. About this time, however, he began to evince a different spirit and nature altogether; he became irritable and moody; at work he would separate himself from his fellow-workers, and when spoken to by them would barely return a civil answer; at home, of course, the change was still more striking. He was cross and would sit moping over the fire all the evening; he rudely repulsed his wife's affectionate efforts to rouse him out of his unhappy humor, and "shut her up" with some snappish expression. When his children ran to meet him, he would push them impatiently aside; altogether his conduct was bearish, disappointing and ill-natured. During four years matters got worse and worse; he often got excited, using violent language to his wife, his children, and the neighbors. Eventually he became maniacal; attempted to kill his wife; assaulted every one who approached him; and even attempted suicide. He then had a succession of epileptic fits and was taken to an asylum. Here he was taciturn, morose and ill-natured; he was averse to doing anything at all, either in the way of work, or joining in amusements. He was suspicious of those about him; moreover, he had a fixed delusion that he was the victim of a conspiracy, on the part of his wife and friends, to deprive him of his liberty and independence; and expressed himself in bitter and resentful terms. A depression of the skull was distinctly traceable both by the eye and by the finger at the point where he sustained the blow. He underwent the operation of trephining, and the depressed portion of bone was removed. After a week or two in bed he was moving about, and a gradual improvement took place. He very soon became a very different person altogether; all his old affection for his wife revived in full force. He became a cheerful, active, lively fellow, never satisfied if he was not doing something. He made friends with the attendants and amongst the patients; and not very long after he was trephined he was discharged sane. He has ever since supported his wife and family. Dr. Skae says: "He has regularly paid visits at about six months intervals to the asylum, generally passing the whole day at it. I have seen him on each occasion, and am satisfied by careful inquiry that he has continued perfectly sane since his discharge four years ago."*

No plainer example, surely, could be wished to show the direct connection of cause and effect, the great deterioration of moral character produced by the physical injury of the supreme nerve centers of the brain. When the cause was taken away the effect went also.

In the morbid conditions of *double consciousness* there is something positive as well as negative; in both these states the vital forces are operating continuously and both have therefore a conviction of continuous existence. In one the identity is laid aside with all the remembrances connected with it, but another is put on, and with the new identity a new memory acts in concert.

A well marked illustration of this is to be found in some cases published by the late Professor Silliman, of Yale College, in the American Journal of Science, and reproduced in the "Cyclopædia of Practical Medicine," Vol. IV., pp. 27, 28, of which a brief abstract is here given.

---

* Journal of Mental Science, January, 1874, Vol. 19, p. 552.

CASE 1. A lady in New England, of respectable family, became subject to paroxysms of delirium, which came on suddenly, and after continuing an indefinite time, went off as suddenly, leaving her mind perfectly rational. It often happened that when she was engaged in conversation, she would stop short in the midst of it, become in a moment delirious, and commence a conversation on some other subject not having the remotest connection with the previous one; nor would she advert to that during her delirium. " When she became natural again she would pursue the same conversation in which she had been engaged during the lucid interval, begining where she left off. To such a degree was this carried, that she would complete an unfinished story or sentence, or even an unfinished word. When the next paroxysm came on she would continue the conversation which she had been pursuing in her preceding paroxysm; so that she appeared as a person might be supposed to do *who had two souls*, each occasionally active and occasionally dormant, and utterly ignorant of what the other was doing." It is evident that this affection was neither delirium in the ordinary acceptation of terms, nor any form of madness, but one of coherent reverie.

CASE 2. An intelligent lady, in the State of New York, undertook a piece of fine needlework, to which she devoted her time almost constantly for many days. Before its completion she became suddenly delirious, and she continued in that state for seven years. She said not a word during that time about her needlework, but, on recovering suddenly from the affection, immediately inquired respecting it.

CASE 3. A farmer, in New England, became

dejected and melancholy under the impression that he
had made an unwise sale of his property.   He was
preparing for the enclosure of a lot of land, and began
with a beetle and wedges to split timber ; at night he
put his tools into a hollow tree and went home.   Here
he was seized with delirium, which continued several
years.   He suddenly recovered, and the first question
which he asked was, whether his sons had brought in
the beetle and wedges?   He appeared to be wholly
unconscious of the lapse of time from the commence-
ment of his attack.   His sons avoided any explanation,
and simply replied that they had been unable to find
the tools.   He immediately arose from his bed, went
into the field, where he had been at work a number of
years before, and found the wedges and the rings of
the beetle where he had left them, the beetle itself
having mouldered away.

The phenomenon of thought alternately interrupted and restored, or of *dipsychia*, as we might term
it in following Professor Silliman's suggestion, though it
reminds us of the old romantic tales of princes laid to
sleep in enchanted castles, is nevertheless confirmed by
sufficient evidence, and may be considered as a well es-
tablished fact.   A notable instance of this description
has been reported in the 'Transactions of the Royal
Society of Edinburgh,' Vol. IX, by Dr. Dyce, and is
cited by Dr. Abercrombie.

The case related by Dr. Dyce is very curious, and
in some of its particulars bears resemblance to the history of Negretti.

Going a step further, let me point out that disease
will sometimes do as plain and positive damage to moral
character as any which direct injury of the brain will do.

A fever has sometimes deranged it as deeply as a blow on the head ; a child's conscience has been clean effaced by a succession of epileptic convulsions, just as the memory is sometimes effaced ; and those who see much of epilepsy know well the extreme but passing moral transformation that occurs in connection with its seizures. The person may be as unlike himself as possible when he is threatened with a fit ; although naturally cheerful, good natured, sociable and obliging, he becomes irritable, surly, and morose, very suspicious, takes offense at the most innocent remark or act, and is apt to resent imaginary offenses with great violence. The change might be compared well with that which happens when a clear and cloudless sky is overcast suddenly with dark and threatening thunder clouds ; and just as the darkly clouded sky is cleared by the thunderstorm which it portends, so the gloomy moral perturbation is discharged and the mental atmosphere cleared by an epileptic fit or a succession of such fits.

In a few remarkable cases however the patient does not come to himself immediately after the fit but is left in a peculiar state of quasi-somnambulism, during which he acts like an automaton, doing strange, absurd, and sometimes even criminal things, without apparently knowing at the time what he is doing, and certainly without remembering in the least what he has done, when he comes to himself. Of excellent moral character habitually, he may turn thief in one of these states, or perpetrate some other criminal offense, whereby he gets himself into trouble with the police.

The following case is taken from a paper read at the Paris International Congress, 1878, by Dr. Echeverria, in which he gave the results of observations on

267 cases of unquestionable Epileptic Insanity forming part of 532 carefully observed cases of epilepsy.

A young man, subject to *petit mal*, in consequence of a fall, one evening after an attack left home, and went in a cabriolet, which he found stopping before a house, to the grave of his father, a mile and a half from Washington, where he gathered flowers to convey to his mother, whom he invited to go for a drive. When she asked how he had obtained the carriage, he answered that he had found it lost in the street. She ordered him to place the horse and carriage instantly in a coach-house, and seek their owner. Instead of obeying he appropriated them, and when the proprietor discovered them he pursued him as a thief. When before the magistrate next day, he could give no account or explanation of his conduct ; in fact it was obliterated from his memory. Some months after when in New York, he left home after one of his seizures, and roving about as a vagabond on the quays, he met an agent who engaged him as a sailor on a vessel about to sail to London. The agreement was duly executed, and after having left with this agent nearly all his money, &c., he embarked. The captain was not long in discovering he was no marine, and finding him very odd, forbade him to mount the masts, and assigned him some light work. Three or four days after, the patient awoke out of this state of unconsciousness, and expressed the greatest astonishment on finding himself on board a vessel, and was unable to give any account of what had occurred. The mother discovered through the police the departure of her son, and took the measures necessary to place him in an asylum. There he had many similar attacks, preceded by nocturnal attacks and *petit mal*, until then unrecognized. In the intervals he was very gentle and reason-able, but during the attacks he was vicious, always in motion, and disposed to be violent.

Dr. Echeverria has yet to find a true case of epi-lepsy without unconsciousness. It is more than patent in the stupor which Delasiauve regards as the character-istic of the disease.

We could not overlook the example cited by Dejœghère, in which the motive and the premeditation are fitly set forth in a case that on the other hand re-mains as a painful record of the punishment of a furious madman, not only unjust, but unmerciful in its inflic-tion :—

Roegiers, aged 30, of strong constitution, was the son of healthy parents. When seven years old he was seized, upon a sudden fright, with an epileptic fit, soon followed by several others, chiefly nocturnal, increasing every time in intensity and duration, until lastly degen-erating into a true rage. Roegiers had a fight with a man named B——. Judged by the Court of Courtrai he was condemned to a few months imprisonment ; he protested his innocence as to the charge brought against him ; furthermore, on leaving the Court he shook hands with B——, assuring him that he entertained no grudge against him, since he could not be held accountable for the wrong decision of the Court. However, it is this very man B—— whom he afterwards intends to kill, and to this effect Roegiers was seen on the day of the mur-der steadily sharpening his knife for several hours on a grindstone, and repeating incessantly : " I shall know how to have you." He then goes out in broad daylight, holding his knife, runs to B——, who lives in a very populous quarter, and boldly enters his house. But

B——, on beholding Roegiers coming with a knife, escapes through the back door. Roegiers chases him, stabs B——'s sister, who endeavored to defend him, and, finally, overtakes him and rushes upon his victim like a tiger. He inflicts upon him a deep wound in the neck, and plunges his nails in it to tear it asunder.

A great crowd hastened to the spot, but the most daring were afraid of going to the rescue of the unfortunate B——. It was not until Roegiers fell down that they took hold of him, and bound him with cords to a wheelbarrow. To every question put to any detail concerning his horrible crime, Roegiers gave always this answer: "Since you make me aware of it, sir, I must needs believe it, but I completely ignore it."

The physician who examined on the mental condition of Roegiers declared that he enjoyed full possession of his reason. Roegiers was condemned to death, but the sentence was commuted to penal servitude for life, and the exposing for one hour. While suffering this last punishment he was seized with such violent convulsions that the executioner was obliged to place him in a chair where he had the greatest difficulty to secure him.[*]

This determination beyond recall of the Court of Courtrai to carry out its sentence to the end has a fitting parallel in Massachusetts.

The case happened in Boston, the Metropolis of New England, about twenty years ago, and the victim of such cold execution of the law was again a wretched young epileptic, subject to diurnal and nocturnal fits; during the latter he would go up the roof of his house, dance in the most dangerous positions, and accomplish

---

[*] "Annales de Medicine" Belges, 1843. Quoted in "La Folie Devant les Tribunaux" par Legrand du Saulle, Paris, 1864, p. 422.

unconsciously such other no less risky feats, which caused his neighbors to call them "dare-devilment." One evening this lad, under the influence of a fit, ran after his sweetheart into the street and took her life with a bread knife he carried home, and of which crime he always protested to have no recollection whatever. Dr. Clement A. Walker, Superintendent of the Lunatic Hospital, Boston, endeavored, unsuccessfully, to satisfy the jury that the boy was an epileptic ; that the homicidal act of violence had been the outcome of epileptic insanity ; that epileptics cannot be held responsible for any act of violence perpetrated during their unconscious automatism which they have no power to control, nor capacity to judge. Consequently he was convicted of manslaughter and sentenced to prison ; but while the judge was uttering the sentence, the boy fell into a violent fit, so violent that several officers—and he was a lad not much over fourteen—failed to control him. A physician was sent for who etherized him, and he was taken back to jail. This physician testified that he thought the fit was feigned, and did not see any good evidence why it was not. About one week after, the prisoner was called for sentence again, when he was brought in by one door, walked through the Court, and taken out by another door. It was ordered by the Court that the prisoner should be sentenced while thus walking through, lest he might be seized with another fit, which exploded twenty-four hours after confinement in prison.

In this singular case, it became a question whether the execution of the law should be carried out in spite of everything, cheating, as it was, the epileptic malady from its attacks, by the strategy of walking the boy across the Court while sentence was pronounced, in utter disregard of the statutory provision by which the prisoner must stand before the judge and jury to hear his sentence, as well as of every humane sentiment of commiseration, to which the violent convulsions experienced by the boy in Court so strongly appealed, and which the judge did not believe to have been simulated, as was demonstrated by the unprecedented and illegal proceeding he authorized in order to prevent a recurrence of a fit.

Dr. David Skae describes the case of a gentleman, afflicted with epilepsy, who came voluntarily under his care, whose violence was most sudden and impulsive, followed by maniacal paroxysm and fury ; "for eight or ten days he spun round and round from left to right— sometimes lying, sometimes sitting, sometimes on his head." While chatting pleasantly over a rubber of whist, he would suddenly perform a somersault over the table, upsetting everything, and, unless forcibly restrained by two or three strong men, assault everybody right and left.

Cases of injury to moral character from sun-stroke are very like those already described. A young officer in the Indian army became insane from sun-stroke and continually complained of his fellow officers poisoning his food. To avoid this annoyance they persuaded him to sell out. He took his passage from Calcutta for England, but the passengers seeing his insanity, refused to travel with him, and the captain landed him at Madras, giving him back half his passage money. After waiting some time he got a passage by a sailing vessel to England, and on his way home he felled the mate of the vessel with a large mallet ; he was put in irons and on his arrival was handed over to the authorities to be tried, being in the meanwhile put in Newgate. On the interposition of his relatives he was released and placed in an asylum. He was generally morose, but joined in the amusements of the other patients, playing cricket, billiards, bowles, and taking long walks, but he never lost sight of the necessity laid upon him to kill somebody.

He left the asylum and has boarded in various houses in the country, under the charge of an attendant, upon whom he has made some murderous assaults.*

The "Neurological Correspondence" of The Journal of Nervous and Mental Diseases, January, 1878, Vol. III, No. 1, contains several interesting notes. Dr. Edward C. Mann read a paper before the Medico-Legal Society of New York, in which he relates the case of a man who had been suffering from sun-stroke, and who took a small quantity of alcohol and then went out for a walk. He met a friend with whom he had been familiar for years, and a discussion arose as to the respective merits of certain politicians, when the argument becoming excited, the man pulled out a revolver and shot his friend. He then went in a confused and dazed state and sat for some hours on a pier near the river; subsequently he went home, burst into tears, and, after informing his wife of the sad occurrence, gave himself up at the police station. There was a total blank in the prisoner's mind in regard to the events immediately preceding the pistol shot, which seemed to have aroused his attention at the time, and he had no recollection of the fact that he had sat on the pier for some time afterwards. There had existed for months previous to the occurrence a profound

---

* Morisonian Lectures on Insanity for 1873, Edited by T. S. Clouston, M. D.

moral or affective derangement, which from its marked periodicity was evidently epileptiform in character, and the sudden homicidal outburst supplied the interpretation of the previously obscure attacks of recurrent derangement. There had evidently been induced, by sun-stroke, an epileptiform neurosis which had been manifesting itself for months, chiefly by irritability, suspicion, moroseness, and perversion of character, with periodic exacerbations of excitement, all foreign to the man previous to the attack of sun-stroke. This epileptic neurosis often exists for a long time in an undeveloped or masked form, and is connected with suicidal and homicidal mania. There is abundant testimony to show that during such seizures persons may perform actions and even speak and answer questions automatically. Moreover, such persons may entertain delusions of fear and persecutions, and commit criminal deeds as a result of such delusions; and when such cases in their terror and distress of mind commit such violent deeds they either experience immediate relief or they continue in a state of excitement unconscious or very imperfectly conscious of the gravity of their acts. When they become conscious again, their memory is apt to be very uncertain as to the preceding events.

Intense cold, it is well known, will affect the mental faculties in a remarkable manner, when the corporeal functions have comparatively suffered less.

Captain Parry relates, that during his voyage of discovery, two young gentlemen, when first they returned on board ship after exposure to intense cold, looked wild, spoke thick and indistinctly, and it was impossible to draw from them a rational answer; the mental powers appeared gradually to revive with the returning circulation ; till then they had the appearance as if they had been drinking too freely.*

Dr. Reich tells us of four boys, from six to ten years of age, who were exposed in a sledge to cold of from sixteen to twenty-two degrees below zero ; and, being suddenly introduced into a room heated by a stove, they showed symptoms of mental derangement, lasting for several hours. There were maniacal excitement, delirium, and halucinations. This condition passed off with a long sleep, and on awakening they retained no recollection whatever of the mental disorder. It is supposed to have been caused by an alteration in the cerebral circulation induced by the rapid change from cold to heat.†

The paroxysms of epilepsy are often preceded by a spectrum; and the state of the brain then existing, whatever it may be, being present in other instances without being followed by the paroxysm, has often been the origin of a belief in supernatural appearances.

Dr. Conolly mentions the case of a gentleman of his acquaintance who in a state approaching to faintness, sometimes induced by cupping, and sometimes by pain, sees the most lovely landscapes displayed before him.‡ The same writer records a case in which an attack of scarlet fever threw all the previous events of a boy's life so much into the shade that they could not be distinctly remembered for many years afterwards ; they were not forgotten, but they were dimly recollected.‖

---

* "Expedition to the North Pole." Vol. I, p. 108.
† "Centralblatt für Nervenheilkunde." No. 6, 1881.
‡ Op. Cit., p. 240.
‖ Op. Cit., p. 236.

One effect of the great plague at Athens is related to have been the impairment of the memory of those who recovered ; so that their friends were often not remembered by them, but were thought to be strangers. In the fever which has been described by certain authors under the name of Calentura, a singular delusion of the senses is said to take place. This affection has been observed in sailors during voyages in hot regions ; the patient mistakes the sea for fields and pastures, representing, perhaps, the scenery of his distant home ; and the patients have been known to walk overboard with this impression.

In consumption, the most fatal of all diseases, there is a state of the brain which prevents much of the suffering which might be expected to arise from the numerous causes of distress which are accumulated in the patient. An immitigable cough, preventing sleep ; a burning fever ; fits of coldness ; profuse and wasting perspiration ; diarrhoea ; frequent sickness ; daily increasing emaciation ; falling hair ; and strength almost hourly diminishing ;—all these lamentable accompaniments or parts of the malady, weigh little on the spirits of the patient, and hopes are entertained, and projects formed, even in the hour of death. Even physicians, to whom all these signs are so familiar as hardly to be mistaken or overlooked, seem to overlook or mistake them in their own persons. M. Bayle, in his excellent work on diseases of the brain, ascribes this effect, which he says he has remarked in three physicians who had died of the malady, to cerebral excitement.

Phthisis being one of the very few organic diseases which often appear in early life, it generally happens that its victims have death set before them before life has lost any of its charm, and whilst every object of human ambition appears in those colors of which time seldom fails to deprive them. But they do not *see* the death that is set before them ; and commonly sink into the grave with hope and promised pleasures still around them.

If we had not hourly proofs of our entire depend- ence on a Governing Power, it might be worth while to remark on the possibility shown to us in the curious in- stances where the delusion is complete, of our being so variously affected by the same external circum- stances as to make our perfect happiness, if it were de- signed that it should be perfect here, quite consistent with the accidents of terrestrial life. No extravagance of imagination is required to admit that the slightest possible change of the mode in which our organization is affected by external agents, might create that happier state to which men look forward amidst the trials of this, but which will probably consist of no less a change of objects than of modes of perceiving them.

There are other diseases which in like manner play havoc with moral feeling. Almost every form of men- tal derangement begins with a moral alienation, slight perhaps at the outset, but soon so great that a prudent, temperate, chaste, and truthful person shall be changed to exactly the opposite of what he was.

This alienation of character continues throughout the course of the disease, and it is frequently found to last for a while after all disorder of intelligence is gone. Indeed the experienced physician never feels confident that the recovery is stable and sure until the person is restored to his natural sentiments and affections. Thus it appears that when the mind undergoes decadence, the moral feeling is the first to suffer ; the highest aquisition of mental evolution, it is the first to witness to mental degeneracy.

One form of mental disease, known as general paralysis, is usually accompanied with a singularly complete paralysis of the moral sense from the outset, and a not uncommon feature of it, very striking in some cases, is a persistent tendency to steal, the person stealing, in a weak minded manner, what he has no particular need of, and makes no use of when he has stolen it.   The victim of this fatal disease is frequently sent to prison and treated as a common criminal, notwithstanding a medical man who knows his business might be able to say with entire certitude that the supposed criminal was suffering from organic disease of the brain, which had destroyed moral sense at the outset, which would go on to destroy all the other faculties of his mind in succession, and which in the end would destroy life itself.   There is no question in such case of moral guilt ; it is not sin, but disease that we are confronted with ; not a theory, but a condition ; and after the victim's death we find the plainest evidence of disease of the brain, which has gone along with the decay of mind.

It can hardly be necessary to remind the reader of the fate of some eminent public characters, men moving in stations of great responsibility, and harassed with the cares of State ; or men engaged in extensive commercial transactions ; or men of studious habits and much ambition, and anxious minds.   Many instances might be mentioned of the fatal end of such persons apparently induced, and in some cases proved to be induced, by slow disease of the brain, or the membranes of the brain, commencing and going on unsus-

pected until it became inconsistent with the perform-
ance of the proper functions of life ; or, until the
long course of self-restraint which has acquired the respect of his fellow creatures suddenly ceases and a man
of high character is reduced to infamy ; or, until producing extreme irritability or melancholy, it causes the individual to die by his own hand. Where no previous
misconduct can be traced, it is more charitable and
generally more just to attribute the misdeed to mental
disturbance arising from positive physical disease.

I need not dwell any longer upon the morality-
sapping effects of particular diseases, but shall simply
call to mind the profound deterioration of moral sense
and will, which is produced by the long-continued and
excessive use of alcohol and opium. There is nowhere
a more miserable specimen of degradation of moral
feeling, and of impotence of will, than the debauchee
who has made himself the abject slave of either of
these pernicious excesses. Insensible to the interests
of his family, to his personal reponsibilities, to the obli-
gations of duty, he is utterly untruthful and untrust-
worthy, and in the worst end there is not a meanness of
pretense, or of conduct, that he will not descend to, not
a lie he will not tell, in order to gain the means to
gratify his overruling craving.

It is not merely that passion is strengthened and
will weakened by indulgence, as a moral effect, but the
alcohol or opium, which is absorbed into his blood, is
carried by it to his brain and acts injuriously upon its
tissues ; the chemist will, indeed, extract alcohol from
the besotted brain of the worst drunkard, as he will detect morphia in the secretions of a person who is taking
large doses of morphia. Seldom, therefore, is it of the

least use to preach reformation to these people until they have been restrained forcibly from their besetting indulgence for a long enough period to allow the brain to get rid of the poison, and its tissues to regain a healthier tone. Too often, it is of little use then; the tissues have been damaged beyond the possibility of complete restoration. Moreover, observation has shown that the drink craving is oftentimes hereditary, so that a taste for the poison is ingrained in the tissues, and is quickly kindled by gratification into uncontrollable desire.

Thus far it appears, then, that moral feeling may be impaired or destroyed by direct injury of the brain, by the disorganizing action of disease, and by the chemical action of certain substances, which, when taken in excess, are poisons to the nervous system.

When we look sincerely at the facts, we cannot help perceiving that it is just as closely dependent upon organization as the meanest function of mind; that there is not an argument to prove the so-called materialism of one part of the mind which does not apply with equal force to the whole mind.

Seeing that we know no more essentially what matter is than what mind is, being unable in either case to go beyond the phenomena of which we have experience, it might be of interest to ask those who cannot conceive that any organization of matter however complex should be capable of such exalted functions as those which are called mental, whether it is really any more conceivable that any organization of matter can be the mechanical instrument of the complex manifestations of an immaterial mind. Is it not just as easy for an omnipotent power to endow matter with mental functions as it is to create an immaterial entity capable of accomplishing them through matter?*

From the time of Locke, the discussions of philosophers have tended to unsettle our notions of matter, and no one is hardy enough, now, to say what it is or what it may not be. It is strangely overlooked by many who write on this matter, that the brain is not a dead instrument, but a living organ, with functions of a higher kind than those of any other bodily organ, inasmuch as its organic nature and structure far surpasses those of any other organ. What, then, are these functions if not mental? No one thinks it necessary to assume an immaterial liver behind the hepatic structure in order to account for its functions. But so far as the nature of nerve and the complex structure of the cerebral convolutions exceed in dignity the hepatic elements and structure, so far must the material functions of the brain exceed those of the liver. Men are not sufficiently careful to ponder the wonderful operations of which matter is capable, or to reflect on the miracles effected by it which are continually before their eyes. Are the properties of a chemical compound less mysterious because of the familiarity with which we handle them? Consider the seed dropped into the ground; it swells with germinating energy; bursts its integuments, sends upward a delicate shoot, which grows into a stem, putting forth in due season its leaves and flowers, until finally a beautiful structure is formed such as Solomon in all his glory could not equal, and all the art of mankind cannot imitate. And yet all these processes are operations of matter; for it is not thought necessary to assume an

* See " Treatise on Christian Doctrine," by John Milton, Vol. 1, pp. 250, 251.

immaterial, or spiritual plant which effects its purposes
through the agency of the material structure which we
observe.*   Surely there are here exhibited properties of
matter wonderful enough to satisfy anyone of the
powers that may be inherent in it.   Are we, then, to
believe that the highest and most complex development
of organic structure is not capable of even more wonderful operations?

Matter, which seems, to common people, so intelli-
gible, is still wrapped in mystery.   We know it only by
its relation to mind or as an assemblage of powers to
awaken certain sensations.

Leaving this inquiry, however, without attempting
to explain the mystery of that which constitutes the
particular nature of matter, on which its properties depend, I pass on to some considerations of the reciprocal
relation of mental function to moral feeling as illustrated
in the development of the human brain.

It is a pretty well accepted scientific doctrine
that our far-distant prehistoric ancestors were a very
much lower order of beings than we are—even if they
did not inherit directly from the monkey; that they
were very much like in conformation, habits, intelligence, and moral feeling, the lowest existing savages; †
and that we have risen to our present level of being by
a slow process of evolution which has been going on
gradually through untold generations.   Whether or not
"through the ages one increasing purpose runs," it is certainly true that "the thoughts of men are widened with
the process of the suns."   Now, when we examine the

* See " Paradise Lost," John Milton, Book V., lines 469–485.

† "Origin of Civilization and the Primitive Condition of Man." Sir
John Lubbock, London, 1870.

brain of the lowest savage—whom we need not be too proud to look upon as our ancestor in the flesh—we find it to be considerably smaller than the ordinary brain of civilized man ; its convolutions, which are the highest nerve centers of mind, are decidedly fewer in number, more simple in character, and more systematic in arrangement.   These are marks of inferiority, for in those things in which it differs from the ordinary brain of civilized man it gets nearer in structure to the still much inferior brain of the monkey ; it represents, we may say, a stage of development in the long distance which has been traversed between the two.   A comparison of the relative brain weights will give a rude notion of the differences ; the brain weight of an average Caucasian male is forty-nine ounces ; that of a negro is forty-four ounces ; and the brains of the Hottentot, Bushman and Australian are, so far as observation goes, of less weight than those of Negroes ; the average weight of the adult male brain is ten per cent. greater than that of the female, and the weight of the male Negro's brain is less than that of the average Caucasian female.*   The brain of the Bushwoman weighed thirty-one and a half ounces ; that of the Hottentot Venus, who was no idiot, was a very little larger.†   Professor Gratiolet carefully figured and described the brain of the Hottentot Venus ; it presented a striking simplicity and regular arrangement of the convolutions of the frontal lobe ; an almost perfect symmetry in the two hemispheres "such as is never exhibited in the normal brains of the Caucasian race," and which involuntarily recalls the regularity and symmetry of the cerebral convolutions

---

* John Thurman, M.D., " Journal of Mental Science," April, 1866.
† Prof. John Marshall, Philosophical Transactions, 1865.

in the lower animals. The brain was palpably inferior
to that of a normally developed white woman; "it
could be compared only with the brain of a white who is
idiotic from arrest of cerebral development."* There
can be no doubt then of a great difference of development between the highest and the lowest existing human
brain.

There can be no doubt, furthermore, that the gross
differences which there are between the size and development of the brain of a low savage, and of an average
Caucasian, go along with great differences of intellectual
and moral capacities; that lower mental function answers to lower cerebral structure. It is a well known
fact that many savages cannot count beyond five,† and
that they have no words in their vocabulary for the
higher qualities of human nature, such as virtue, justice,
humanity, and their opposites, vice, injustice, and cru-
elty, or for the more abstract ideas. The native Australian, for example, who is in the case, having no words
for justice, love, mercy, and the like, would not in the
least know what remorse meant; if anyone showed it
in his presence, he would think, probably, that he had
got a bad headache. He has no words to express the
higher sentiments and thoughts, because he has never
felt and thought them, and has never, therefore, had
the need to express them; ‡ he has not in his inferior

---

* Transactions of the Anthropological Society, Paris, 1861.

† Brett, " History of the British Colonies in the West Indies." 4th ed.,
London, 1887.

‡ True love, observes Sir John Lubbock, is almost unknown amongst
the lowest races, and marriage in its lowest phases is by no means a matter
of affection and companionship. Among the Koussa Kaffirs, Lichtenstein
asserts that there is no feeling of love in marriage. In North America the
Tinné Indians had no word for "dear" or "beloved," and the Algonquin

brain the nervous substrata which should minister to such sentiments and thoughts, and cannot have them in his present state of social evolution, any more than he could make a particular movement of his body if the proper muscles were wanting. Nor could any amount of training in the world, we may be sure, ever make him equal in this respect to the average Caucasian, any more than it could add substance to the brain of a small-headed idiot and raise it to the ordinary level. Were anyone, indeed, to make the experiment of taking the young child of an Australian savage and of bringing it up side by side with an average European child, taking pains to give them exactly the same education in every respect, he would certainly have widely different results in the end; in the one case he would have to do with a well-organized instrument, ready to give out good intellectual notes, and a fine harmony of moral feeling when properly handled; in the other case, an imperfectly organized instrument, from which it would be out of the power of the most patient and skillful touch to elicit more than a few feeble intellectual notes, and a very rude and primitive sort of moral feeling, a little better feeling, certainly, than that of its fathers, but still most primitive; for many savages regard as virtues most of the big vices and crimes, such as theft, rape, murder, at any rate, when they are practiced at the expense of neigh-

---

language is stated to have contained no verb meaning "to love," so that when the Bible was translated by the missionaries into that language, it was necessary to invent a word for that purpose. He cites a French writer to show that the Samoyedes of Siberia show little affection for their wives and "*daignent à peine leur dire une parole de douceur.*" Many other instances might be adduced to illustrate this remarkable fact, but these are sufficient to show that in one very important circumstance at any rate the early races did not approach the more civilized nations.

boring tribes.* Their moral feeling, such as it is, is extremely circumscribed, being limited in ·application to the tribe. In civilized society we have, happily, got a step further than that, since we are not as savages are, and our forefathers probably were, divided into a multitude of tribes eager to injure and even extirpate one another from motives of tribal patriotism.† No doubt we have reached a much higher pitch of moral feeling now, but there is plainly room yet for a wider expansion, and mankind seems to be far off the gaol of its high calling, so long as divided into jealous and hostile nations it suffers national divisions to limit the application of moral feeling.

Now, what do the discoveries of science warrant us to conclude respecting the larger and more complex brain of the civilized man, and its higher capacities of thought and feeling? They teach us this; that it has reached its higher level not by any sudden and big creative act, nor by a succession of small creative acts, but by the slow and gradual operation of processes of natural evolution going on through countless ages. Each new insight into natural phenomena on the part of man,

---

* The wife of an Australian savage having died of some disease, he informed Dr. Lander that he would go and kill a woman of a distant tribe, so that his wife's spirit might have rest. Forbidden imperatively to do so, and threatened with imprisonment if he did, he became wretched and wasted away; but he disappeared eventually, and was absent for some time. When he re-appeared he was in good condition, for he had succeeded in killing a woman; his sorrow because of a sacred duty omitted had disappeared, his tribal moral feeling was satisfied, and his bodily nutrition sympathized with the restored animation of his mind.—*American Journal of Insanity*, July, 1871.

† The story of Jael and Sisera is instructive in this respect; the light in which she was regarded for her abuse of the sacred rite of Eastern hospitality showing the limited range of moral feeling at that time.—*Judges*, v. 24-27.

each act of wiser doing founded on truer insight, each bettered feeling which has been developed by wiser conduct, has tended to determine by degrees a corresponding structural change of the brain, which has been transmitted, as an innate endowment, to succeeding generations, just as the acquired habit of a parent animal becomes sometimes the instinct of its offspring, and the accumulated results of these slow and minute gains transmitted by hereditary action, have culminated in the higher cerebral organization in which they now are, as it were, capitalized. Thus the added structure embodies in itself the superior intellectual and moral capabilities of abstract reasoning and moral feeling, which have been the slow acquisitions of the ages, and it gives them out again in its functions when it discharges its functions rightly. If one of our remote pre-historic ancestors were to come to life among us now, we should have more or less of an imbecile, who could not compete on equal terms with other persons, but must perish, unless charitably cared for, just as the low savage whose brain is destitute of the higher nervous substrata of thought and feeling perishes, when he comes in contact and competition with the white man. The only way in which the native savage can be raised to the level of civilized thought and feeling must be, if it shall be, by cultivation through many generations, by a process of evolution similar to that which lies back between our savage ancestors and us.

That is one aspect of the operation of natural law in human events, the operation of the law of heredity in development in carrying mankind forward, that is, to a higher level of being. It teaches us plainly enough that the highest qualities of mind bear witness to the reign of law in nature as certainly as do the lowest prop-

erties of matter, and that if we are to go on progressing
in time to come it must be by the observation of, and
obedience to, the laws of development.

There is, however, another important aspect of the
law of heredity which it concerns us to bear sincerely in
mind, its operation in working out human degeneracy,
in carrying mankind downward, that is, to a lower level
of being. It is certain that man may degenerate as well
as develop; that he has been doing so both as nation
and individual, ever since we have records of his doings
on earth. In many regions of the globe there have
been a succession of partial civilizations that have been
followed by periods of barbarism; some of the savages
of to-day are the heirs of higher races that have perished. There is a broad and easy way of dissolution,
national, social, and individual, which is the opposite of
the steep and narrow way of evolution. In the flowing
tide of progress there are innumerable ebbing waves.
Now what it behooves us to realize distinctly is that
there is not anything more miraculous about the degeneration or extinction of a nation, or a family, than there
is about its rise and development; that both are the
work of natural law. A nation does not sink into decadence, I presume, so long as it keeps fresh those virtues of character through which it became great among
nations; it is when it suffers them to be eaten away by
luxury, corruption, and other enervating vices, that it
undergoes that degeneration of character which prepares
and makes easy its overthrow. In like manner a family
reckless of the laws of physical and moral hygiene, may
go through a process of degeneracy until it becomes extinct. What we call mental derangement is truly in
most cases a form of human degeneracy, a phase in the

working out of it ; and if this degeneracy were suffered
to take its course through generations the natural termi-
nation would be extinction of the family. If a man
will but make himself the subject of serious scientific
study, he shall find that this working out of degeneracy
through generations affords him a rational explanation
of most of those evil impulses of the heart which he
has been content to attribute to the wiles and instiga-
tions of the devil ; that the evil spirit which has taken
possession of the wicked man is often the legacy of
parental or ancestral error, misfortune, or wrong doing.

Let us take for the purpose of illustrating by example the nature and bearing of this scientific study a
case which every physician who has had much experience must have been asked some time or other to
consider and advise about ; a quite young child which
is causing its parents alarm and distress by the precocious display of vicious desires and tendencies of all
sorts that are quite out of keeping with its tender
years, and by the utter failure of either precept, or example, or punishment, to imbue it with good feeling
and with the desire to do right. It may not be no-
tably deficient in intelligence ; on the contrary it may
be capable of learning quickly, when it likes, and extremely cunning in lying, in stealing, in gratifying
other perverse inclinations; and it cannot be said not
to know right from wrong, since it invariably eschews
the right and chooses the wrong, showing an amazing
acuteness in escaping detection, and the punishment
which follows detection. It is in truth, congenitally
conscienceless, by nature destitute of moral sense, and
actively imbued with immoral sense. Now this unfortunate creature is of so tender an age that the theory

of satanic agency is not thought to offer an adequate explanation of its evil impulses; in the end everybody who has to do with it feels that it is not responsible for its vicious conduct, perceives that punishment does not, and cannot, in the least, reform it, and is persuaded that there is some native defect of mind which renders it a proper case for medical advice.

To show that this portrait is no exaggerated fancy sketch let me relate a case described by Mr. Haslam— a boy ten years of age who was sent to the Bethlehem Hospital to be cared for.   The history of the case is as follows :

The parents are persons of sound mind and they do not remember any branches of their respective families to have been in any manner disordered in their intellects.   The subject of the present relation was their eldest son ; the second child was of a disposition remarkably mild ; and the youngest, a boy of about two and a half years, was distinguished by the irritability and impatience of his temper.   At the age of two years the subject of the present relation became so mischievous and uncontrollable that he was sent from home to be nursed by his aunt.   In this situation he continued until he was nearly nine years old ; the creature of volition and the terror of the family ; at this time the advice of a physician was sought. Different systems of management were adopted, indulgence in every wish and correction for each individual perverseness, or impropriety of conduct.   He would neither dress nor undress himself, though capable of both ; when his hands were at liberty he tore his clothes ; he broke everything that was presented to him, or came within his reach, and frequently refused to take food. He gave answers only to such questions as pleased him, and acted in opposition to every direction. His aunt exercised this plan for several months, but perhaps not to the extent laid down; for it may be presumed that after a few flagellations her humanity prevailed. He was of a very healthy appearance, and his head was well formed. His tongue was unusually thick, though his articulation was perfectly distinct. His countenance is described as decidedly "maniacal," a complex term for many ideas not very easy to be defined. His stature for his age was short, but he was well compacted and possessed great bodily strength. His skin was smooth and clear, though somewhat deficient in sensibility; his pulse was natural, appetite good but not inordinate. He slept soundly, and seemed to require a considerable duration of sleep, though he often awoke as if suddenly alarmed. He had a very retentive memory, and had made as great proficiency in speech as the generality of boys at his age. Few circumstances appeared to give him pleasure, but he would describe very correctly anything which had delighted him. He had been several times at school but as he lacked the power of continued attention, and was only attracted by fits and starts, he was the hopeless pupil of many masters, distinguished for their patience and rigid discipline; it may, therefore, be concluded that from these gentlemen he derived all the benefits which could result from privations to his stomach and from the application of the rod to the more delicate parts of his skin.

Mr. Haslam says: "On the first interview I had with him he contrived after two or three minutes' acquaintance to break a window and tear the frill of my shirt. He was an unrelenting foe to all china, glass, and crockery ware ; whenever they came within his reach he shivered them instantly. In walking the street the keeper was compelled to take the wall as he uniformly broke the windows if he could get near them, and his operation was performed so dextrously and with such safety to himself that he never cut his fingers. To tear lace and destroy the finer textures of female ornament seemed to gratify him exceedingly, and he seldom walked out without finding an occasion of indulging this propensity. He never became attached to any inferior animal ; to these creatures his conduct was that of a brute ; he oppressed the feeble and avoided the society of those more powerful than himself. When he was spoken to he usually said : ' Now I will look unpleasant.' The usual games of children afforded him no amusement ; whenever boys were at play he never joined them ; he appeared incapable of forming a friendship with anyone ; he felt no consideration for sex, and would as readily kick or bite a girl as a boy. Of kindness shown him he was equally insensible ; he would receive an orange as a present, and afterwards throw it in the face of the donor. To the man who looked after him he appeared to entertain something like an attachment ; when this person went out of the room he raised a loud outcry, and said : ' What will become of me if he goes away ? I like him, for he carries the cane which makes me a good boy.' The man seemed to be of a different opinion, however, for he said, when he grew older he should be afraid to continue with him, as he was persuaded the boy would destroy him, whenever he found the means and opportunity. Of his own disorder he was sometimes sensible ; he would often express a wish to die, for, he said, 'God had not made him like other children.' During the time he remained at Bethlehem, I conducted him through the hospital and pointed out to him several patients who were chained in their cells ; he discovered no fear or alarm ; and when a mischievous maniac, who was more strictly confined than the rest, was shown him, he said : 'This would be the right place for me.' Considering the duration of his insanity, and being ignorant of any means by which he was likely to recover, he was returned to his friends after remaining a few weeks in London."*

Where, then, is the fault that a human being is born into the world who will go wrong, nay, who must go wrong, in virtue of a bad organization ? How comes it that an individual capable of looking before and after, remembering the retribution of past sin and the Nemesis that awaits a future wrong doing is so forgetful of true self interest as to yield to evil impulses ? And whence do these impulses come ? One thing is certain, Moral Philosophy cannot penetrate the hidden springs of feeling and impulse, they lie deeper than it can reach, for they lie in the physical constitution of the individual, and going still farther back, perhaps in his organic antecedents. Moral Philosophy may make its hard and fast lines, and lay down abstract propositions concerning the power of will in the conduct of life, but when we have to do with concrete cases it is plain that no such definite lines can be applied, and that abstract propositions are only true of a certain proportion of mankind. Moreover, it appears also that those of whom they are true, have much less merit in the matter, and those of whom they are not true, much less blame than moral philoso-

* "Observations on Madness." John Haslam, London, 1809, Page 198.

phers are apt to imagine and inculcate.   The fate of inheritance, which constitutes the misfortune of the latter,
constitutes also the virtue of the former.   His father
and mother, his grandfather and grandmother, are latent
or declare themselves in him ; and it is on the lines laid
down in his nature that his development has proceeded.
Humanity is contained in the individual ; whatever act
of vice, folly, crime, or madness one man has perpetrated, each man has in him the potentiality of perpe-
trating.   It is not by virtue of education so much as by
virtue of inheritance that he is brave or timid, generous
or selfish, prudent or reckless, boastful or modest, quick
or placid in temper ; the ground tone of his character is
original in him, and it colors all the subsequently
formed emotions and their sympathetic ideas.   As in
one word ages of human culture are summed up,*
so in one mortal are summed up generations of human
existence ; in his nature as in his knowledge man is the
inheritor of the acquisitions of the past, the heir of all
the ages.

Instead of regarding the mind as it were from the
center, one should approach the consideration of it by
degrees from the circumference ; instead of starting
with man as the immediate object of philosophy, let
us start from the outer inert world, at the disposal of
physical and chemical forces ; what do we see result ?
Another world where the forms individualize themselves
and of which the continued mobility attests the presence of new agents !   Minerals, plants, animals detach
themselves, and appear to us as the steps of evolution
in nature rising higher and higher.   And man ! he ap-

* "Some Lessons of Antiquity."   An address delivered at the Man-
sion House, 23d of February, 1889, by Prof. F. Max Muller.

pears at the summit of this vast series, species among
the species, individual in his species. But between
the species and the individual is there not yet something? Between the human type, as it can be anatom-
ically defined, and this same type as it manifests itself
in each one of us, is there not a gap? And the gap
is filled by the very history of the human species; for
we pertain to races, to varieties of the human race,
and we all accept the heritage of a long past; we
have, if we may be permitted to employ the expression,
a historical mind—we are one of the links of a long
chain.

However great may be the discoveries that are yet
to be made, it is an assured principle that humanity
has not always been exactly similar to itself. The ideas
which constitute our most precious patrimony have had
their history; civilizations which are nothing else than
the aggregate of ideas dominant at a certain epoch,
and in certain countries, have not been servile copies
one of another; mental enlightenment has changed its
place; but at the same time it has increased. This
historic mind of which the first impulses and the most
spontaneous testimony remains lost in the darkness of
the past, develops itself from age to age, from nation
to nation; never definitely fixing itself upon one particular religion, æsthetics, or philosophy; the mind,
wafted by a favorable wind, seeks new shores, and the
world seems to be colored with clearer light. These
periods of excitement are never wasted; nothing is lost;
nothing is useless; the impulse once given diffuses itself,
extends itself, and never stops. If we take the words
which express the thoughts of a high mental culture
and trace their origin and the gradual development of

their meanings, what a succession of human experiences, rising in complexity is displayed ! There is not an abstract term that does not mean generations of human culture. Let us take in like manner the human being and trace back through the long record of ages the steps of his genesis, or examine rather the resolution of his essential human nature into its lower elements, as exhibited in the degenerate acts of this child, and we shall cease to be surprised at phenomena which the young creature never could have acquired, and which, so far as its conscious life is concerned, appears strangely precocious and inexplicable. We are witnesses of a retrograde metamorphosis of humanity, of the undoing of what has been done through ages, of the formless ruin of carefully fashioned form.

We can seldom find the exact cause and trace definitely the mode of its operation ; the study is much too complex and difficult for such exactness at present, but we shall not fail to discover the broad fact of the frequency of mental degeneracy in the direct line of the child's ancestors. The influence of systematic culture upon anyone is no doubt great, but that which determines the limit, and even in some degree the nature of the effect of culture, that which forms the foundation upon which all the modifications of art must rest, is the inherited nature.

Many an experience in life teaches the individual who has had the blessing of a good parentage, how incalculable is his debt ; when compelled to act at critical moments, or under difficult and trying circumstances, to which he was not consciously equal, or under great temptation to do wrong, or in any other case in which his art has failed him, he shall have cause to bless the nature which he has inherited, to give thanks for the reserve force of a sound and vigorous character which his parents have endowed him with, and which has stood him in good stead, and inspired him, as his leisurely consideration proves, to do rightly when he knew not what he was doing. Better than all his pastors and masters can teach him, it will enable him to meet his last fate with becoming dignity, in the hour of death and in the day of judgment.

The individual's nature is beneath his art; if sound it will come to his rescue when culture fails him; if unsound it will overthrow him in the hour of trial in spite of culture.*

Instances sometimes occur in young children of blind destructive impulse, or even of persistent homicidal desire. Romberg met with a child six years old which suffered from attacks of blind destructive impulse, in which it smashed to pieces whatever it could, rushed into the street with a knife in its hand and could scarce be restrained.†

In younger children of three or four years old, attacks of shrieking, wild refractoriness, rage, biting, and destructive propensities, which occur periodically, are sometimes met with. And if anyone should think that these are instances of early depravity what will he say to the case of a child raving mad immediately after birth. Chrichton quotes such a case. When four days old he possessed so much strength in his legs and arms, that four women could, at times with difficulty restrain him. These paroxysms either ended with an inde-

* "Man fancies that he determines his life, that he guides himself, and all the while his nature is an irresistable part of his destiny."—GOETHE's *Egmont.*

† Deutsche Klinik, 1851, p. 178.

scribable laughter, for which no evident reason could be observed, or else he tore in anger everything near him, which he could tear, clothes, linen, bed furniture, and even thread, when he could get hold of it. When he began to have teeth, he died.* The case seems to be an example of sensorial insanity, and is not unlike those cases in which convulsions prove fatal to young children. The earliest acts of the new-born child are reflex, and these, when there is a morbid condition of nerve element, may become convulsions. To the reflex acts follow consensual or sensational acts ; and these, when there is a morbid state of the sensory ganglia, became the tearing, biting, and unnatural laughter of the insane infant. In the animal, where the nervous center of idea is but imperfectly developed, the insanity is also sensorial.

A child may be afflicted also at an early age with a persistent morbid homicidal desire. A well-known case is recorded by Esquirol in which a girl aged seven and a half years manifested a fixed desire to kill her stepmother, who had always treated her kindly. The grandmother had, in the child's hearing, expressed her dissatisfaction with its father's second marriage, without foreseeing the effect which might be produced on a child then only two years old.† To sensational respondence to external nature succeeds, in the order of mental development, ideational reaction ; and when ideational activity is first beginning, it is not difficult to implant an idea which may long abide.

Another case of a girl, aged seven years and a half, who made repeated attempts to injure and kill her

* Op., Cit., Vol. II, Appendix, p. 355.
† "Traité des Maladies Mentales," Tome II., p. 115.

mother, is related by Parent-Duchâtelet;* the morbid
tension of the ganglionic cells had been brought about
in this case by a well-recognized cause of disturbance at
all ages.

How are we to account for those cases of *juvenile*
suicide so often recorded, where the dreadful propensity
is excited by the most trivial causes? Medical literature
is rich in such examples.

Physiologically, psychologically and pathologically,
we are brought back to the same conclusion, namely,
that the unconscious action of the organism is a deeper
fact than its conscious action, that the real conditions
of mental action must be investigated in regions of
which introspective consciousness gives no account.
What real meaning is there in saying, that "man is conscious to himself of faculties not comprised within the
chain of physical necessity," when a blow on the head,
or the virus of a fever, or any such physical cause, in a
moment lays low the highest faculties of the proudest
metaphysician? The unrelenting circle of necessity en-
compasses all. One may go his destined course with
tranquil resignation, and another may fret and fume,
but willingly or unwillingly both must go. The cage
may be a larger or a smaller one, but the bars are always there. "Where wast thou when I laid the foundations of the earth? Canst thou bind the sweet influences of Pleiades, or loose the bands of Orion? Canst
thou bring forth Mazzaroth in his season? Or canst
thou gird Arcturus with his sons? Then Job answered
and said: 'Behold, I am vile; what shall I answer
thee? I will lay my hand upon my mouth.'" On what

* "Annales d' Hygiène publique et de Médicine legale," Tome VII., p.
173, et suiv, Paris, 1832.

foundation can mental science surely rest save on a careful induction from all available facts, whether they are
called physiological or psychical ?   " Happy they," says
Goethe, " who soon detect the chasm that lies between
their wishes and their powers."

One of the most extraordinary instances of the operation of this law in working out moral degeneracy
without any perceivable weakening of the intellectual
faculty is the case of Servin, described in the Duke of
Sully's " Memoirs of Henry IV. of France," and which
Dr. Rush regarded as a case of "universal moral derangement."

Sully says :—" Just before my departure from Calais,
old Servin came and presented his son to me, and
begged I would use my endeavors to make him a man of
some worth and honesty ; but he confessed it was what
he dared not hope, not through any want of understanding or capacity in the young man, but from his natural
inclination to all kinds of vice.   The old man was in the
right ; for what he told me having excited my curiosity
to gain a thorough knowledge of young Servin, I found
him to be at once both a wonder and a monster ; for I
can give no other idea of that assemblage of the most
excellent and most pernicious qualities.   Let the reader
represent to himself a man of genius so lively, and an
understanding so extensive, as rendered him acquainted
with almost everything that could be known ; of so vast
and ready a comprehension that he immediately made
himself master of whatever he attempted, and of so pro-
digious a memory that he never forgot what he had once
learned.   He possessed all parts of philosophy and the
mathematics, particularly fortification and drawing ; even
in theology he was so well skilled that he was an excel-

lent preacher whenever he had a mind to exert that talent, and an able disputant for and against the reformed religion indifferently.   He not only understood Greek, Hebrew, and all the languages which we call learned, but also all the different jargons or modern dialects; he accented and pronounced them so naturally, and so perfectly imitated the gestures and manners both of the several nations of Europe, and the particular provinces of France, that he might have been taken for a native of all or any of these countries; and this quality he applied to counterfeit all sorts of persons, wherein he succeeded wonderfully; he was, moreover, the best comedian and greatest droll that, perhaps, ever appeared; he had a genius for poetry, and had written many verses; he played upon almost all instruments, was a perfect master of music, and sang most agreeably and justly; he likewise could say mass, for he was of a disposition to do, as well as to know, all things; his body was perfectly well suited to his mind, he was light, nimble, dextrous, and fit for all exercises; he could ride well, and in dancing, wrestling, and leaping, he was admired; there are no games of recreation that he did not know; and he was skilled in almost all mechanic arts.   But now for the reverse of the medal.   Here it appeared that he was treacherous, cruel, cowardly, deceitful; a liar, a cheat, a drunkard and glutton; a sharper in play, immersed in every species of vice, a blasphemer, an atheist; in a word, in him might be found all the vices contrary to nature, honor, religion and society; the truth of which he evinced with his latest breath, for he died in the flower of his age, in a low house, perfectly corrupted by his debaucheries, and expired with a glass in his hand, cursing and denying God." *

---

* " Memoirs of the Duke of Sully, Prime Minister to Henry the Great," Vol. III., p. 35.

If it be a question in this instance whether controllable vice, or uncontrollable impulse, would the more properly characterize the case of this young man, we may, I think, reasonably conclude that there was some constitutional peculiarity. Whether or not we hesitate to pronounce him wholly irresponsible, we may agree with Rush, that "such persons are, in a pre-eminent degree, objects of compassion, and that it is the business of medicine to aid law in preventing and curing their moral alienation of mind." (Op. cit., p. 358.)

It is, indeed, most certain that men are not bred well or ill by accident any more than animals are; but while most persons are ready to acknowledge this fact in a general way, very few pursue the admission to its exact and vigorous consequences, and fewer still suffer it to influence their conduct.

An extraordinary example of the perpetuation of the criminal class by heredity is afforded by the history of the infamous Jukes family, whose pedigree has been made out with singular care, notwithstanding the vagrant habits, illegitimate unions, and extreme untruthfulness, to which this particular class of humanity is disposed. It has been traced during no less than seven generations, and is the subject of an elaborate memoir printed in the Thirty-first Annual Report of the Prison Association of New York, 1876. It includes no less than 540 individuals of Jukes blood, of whom a frightful number degraded into criminality, pauperism, or disease. It is difficult to summarize the results in a few plain figures, but those respecting the fifth generation, through the eldest of the five prolific daughters of the man who is the common ancestor of the race, may be stated.

The total number of these was 123, of whom thirty-eight came through an illegitimate granddaughter, and eighty-five through legitimate grandchildren. Out of the thirty-eight, sixteen have been in jail, sixteen for heinous offenses, one of these having been committed no less than nine times; eleven others led openly disreputable lives, or were paupers; the history of three had not been traced, and only four are known to have done well.

The great majority of the women consorted with criminals. As to the eighty-five legitimate descendants, they were less flagrantly bad, for only five of them had been in jail, and only thirteen had been paupers.

Now, the ancestor of all this mischief, who was born about the year 1730, is described as having been a jolly, companionable sort of man, a hunter, and a fisher, a hard drinker, averse to steady labor, but working hard and idling by turns, and who had numerous illegitimate children, whose issue has not been traced.

He was, in fact, a somewhat good specimen of a half-savage, without any seriously criminal instincts. The girls were apparently attractive, marrying early and sometimes not badly; but the gypsy-like character of the race was unsuited to success in a civilized country. So the descendants went to the bad, and such hereditary moral weaknesses as they may have had, rose to the surface and worked their mischief without check. Cohabitating with criminals, and being extremely prolific, the result was the production of a stock exceeding 500 in number, of a prevalent criminal type. Through disease and intemperance the breed is now rapidly diminishing; the infant mortality has of late been horrible, but fortunately the women of the present generation

bear usually fewer children, and many of them are altogether childless. The criminal classes contain a considerable portion of epileptics, and other persons of
instable, emotional temperaments, subject to nervous
explosions which burst out at intervals and relieve the
system. Their instability of nervous action, irregulari-
ties of bodily temperature, mobile intellectual activity,
and extraordinary oscillations between opposed emotional states give rise to manifestations of extreme
piety and of extreme vice. These unfortunate beings
see no incongruity between the pious phrases which
they pour out at one moment and their vile and ob-
scene language in the next; neither do they show
repentance for past misconduct when they are convicted
of crimes, however abominable they may be. They are
creatures of the moment, possessing no inhibitory check
upon their desires and emotions, which drive them
headlong hither and thither. From Max Jukes de-
scended in seventy-five years, 200 thieves and murder-
ers, 280 invalids attacked by blindness, idiocy, or consumption, 90 prostitutes, and 300 children who died
prematurely. The various members of the family cost
the State more than a million dollars.*

The inheritance of evil tendencies was strikingly
exhibited in the history of a family reported by Miss
Schuyler, President of the New York State Charity
Aid Society. (New York Times, March 8th, 1878.)
"Margaret," the "mother of criminals," left behind her
"a long train of diseases, weaknesses, bad habits, cor-
rupt and morbid passions, physical and moral degeneracy,
and open crimes which can never be measured by human
eye.

* *Dugdale :* " The Jukes."

The female children of the line became mothers, in their teens, of illegitimate children ; the boys were thieves and vagrants as by a law of nature, as soon as they could exercise any activity. . . . . . . The children grew up in nurseries of crime and became, of course, paupers or worse. The stronger and bolder lived by thieving, or committed burglary, robbery or murder. Crime and indulgence gradually caused the degeneracy of some and they became epileptics, lunatics, and idiots. . . . . . . Some of this miserable breed reached the age of ninety years, and some of the women had at least twenty children. The stock of this race of criminals was preserved by intermarriage with fresh and vigorous families of ruffians. The total number of the race was seven hundred, mainly paupers, beggars, prostitutes and criminals."

It is a great pity that men cannot be brought to realize the important truth, that an inheritance far better than land or wealth, which they may leave to their children, is that of a good nature—the "confidence of a good descent." It is a great blessing, however, that when men neglect this truth, nature takes the matter out of their hands, and, with the determination that progress shall not be frustrated by human follies and vices, puts a stop to propagation by sterility and idiocy.

The hereditary kinship which is sometimes traceable between crime and insanity I do not purpose to set forth in detail ; the subject is discussed fully by Dr. Prosper Lucas, in the well-known classic, *Traité philosophique et physiologique de l'Hérédite Naturelle ;* but to make clear what I mean I will give one or two illustrations. Of five children from an insane mother and

a drunken father, one was suicidal, two suffered imprisonment for crimes, one daughter was insane, the other was
imbecile.　In Haslam's Work on Madness, under the
section, "Influence of Heredity," may be found this
record :—

M. H.　Her father had been several times insane ;
her mother was likewise so afflicted a few months before
her death.　Afterwards her father married a woman
perfectly sane by whom he had three children, two
female and one male ; both the females were melan-
cholic, the male was a vicious character and had been
transported.　M. H. has had ten children, three have
died with convulsions, the eldest girl is epileptic.

M. Morel, of Rouen, relates the history of one
family which may be shortly summed up thus :—

FIRST GENERATION.—Immorality,　Alcoholic Excess,
　　Moral Brutishness.

SECOND GENERATION.—Hereditary drunkenness, Mani-
　　acal attacks, General Paralysis.

THIRD GENERATION.—Sobriety, Hypochondria, Lype-
　　mania, Systematic Delirium, Homicidal tenden-
　　cies.

FOURTH GENERATION.—Feeble intelligence, Stupidity,
　　First attack of Mania at 16, Transition to com-
　　plete Idiocy ; probable extinction of the race.*

The case of Christiana Edmonds is a notable
one :—

She was convicted of murder, afterwards reprieved
and sent to an asylum; her brother died epileptic and
idiotic; her sister suffered from mental excitement, and
once attempted to throw herself out of a window ; her

* Traité des Dégénérescences, de l'Espèce Humaine. B. A. Morel,
Paris, 1857. Page 125.

mother's father died paralyzed and childish ; a cousin on
the same side was imbecile ; she had herself been subject to somnambulism in childhood, had suffered from
hysteria later in life, and had finally had an attack of
hemiplegia ; and at the time of her trial her face drawn
to one side showed the effect of the hemiplegic attack
from which she suffered.

Dr. Maudsley, whose testimony, as an expert in
the case, is given in the " Journal of Mental Science,"
says : " I had more than an hour's conversation with her
in Newgate, and, at the end of it, two convictions were
firmly planted in my mind ; the first that she had no real
moral appreciation of the nature of her crime, and no
shadow of a feeling of remorse in regard to it, the second that she would have poisoned a whole city full of
people, if it had lain in her way to do so, without
hesitation, compunction, or remorse. Nevertheless, her
intellect was acute, certainly above the average, and
showed no signs of disorder. I could only regard her
case as a strong confirmation of an opinion I have else-
where expressed, and which I believe to be a just conclusion from facts ; namely, that one occasional result
of descent from an insane family is a nature entirely
destitute of moral sense—congenitally defective in that
respect—whereby the individual is as insensible to the
moral relations of life, as a person color blind is to certain colors."*

One example more shall suffice to exhibit the alli-
ance between degenerate types ; it shows the effect of
crime in one generation of a family upon the mental
organization of the following generations.

While the Reign of Terror was going on during

* " Journal of Mental Science." Vol. xviii, p. 409.

the first French Revolution, an innkeeper profited by the critical situation in which many nobles of his commune found themselves, to decoy them into his house, where he was believed to have robbed and murdered them. His daughter, having quarrelled with him, denounced him to the authorities, who put him on his trial, but he escaped conviction from lack of proof. She committed suicide subsequently; one of her brothers had nearly murdered her with a knife, and another brother hanged himself; her sister was paroxysmally violent; her daughter, in whom the degenerate line approached extinction, became completely deranged and was sent to an asylum.*

Here, then, is just the sort of pedigree which we really want—if we are to judge of the worth of a family,—the hereditary line of its vices, virtues, and diseases.

FIRST GENERATION.—Acute Intelligence, Murder and Robbery, Absence or Destruction of Moral Sense.

SECOND GENERATION.—Suicide, Homicidal violence and suicide, Epilepsy, Imbecility, Mania.

THIRD GENERATION.—Mania.

It may be said that this was an extreme and exceptional case; but it is on that account better fitted to produce an impression; and it must be remembered that the laws by which its results were worked out are laws which are continually at work in accomplishing less striking results, and that so-called exceptional cases in science are when rightly studied exceptionally useful in helping us to discover the laws for which we are searching. What we wish to prove is that the moral element

---

* Moreau, " La Psychologie Morbide," p. 359.

is an essential part of a complete and sound character, in the present state of human evolution. He who is destitute of moral sense is to that extent a defective be- ing; he marks the beginning of race degeneracy; and if better influences do not intervene to check or neutralize the morbid tendency, his children will exhibit a further degeneracy and be actually morbid varieties. What shall be the particular outcome of the morbid strain . —whether vice, or crime, or madness—will, of course, depend on the circumstances of life; the inborn fact counts for much, but not for everything, in the result. It, or the potentiality of it, is inherited by most per- sons, though some appear to be born without it; it is developed by culture, decays by disuse, and is perverted or destroyed by disease.

"Crime," says Dr. Maudsley, "is not always a simple affair of yielding to an evil impulse, or a vicious passion, which might be checked were ordinary control exercised ; it is clearly sometimes the result of an actual neurosis which has close relations of nature and de- scent to other neuroses ; and this neurosis is the physical result of physiological laws of production and evolution. The criminal psychosis which is the mental side of the neurosis is for the most part an intractable malady, pun- ishment being of no avail to produce a permanent re- formation. A true reformation would be a *re*forming of the individual nature ; and how can that which has been forming through generations be *re*formed within the period of a single life ? 'Can the Ethiopian change his skin, or the leopard his spots ?'" *

It may be set down then as a fact of observation,

---

* Address to the Psychological Section, British Medical Association, August 7, 1872, Henry Maudsley, M. D

that mental degeneracy in one generation is sometimes the evident cause of an innate deficiency or absence of moral sense in the next generation. The child bears the burden of its ancestral infirmities or wrong doings. It was this avenging law of heredity by which guilt brings after it its punishment on earth, and the children expiate the sins or errors of the parents, that under the name of fate or destiny often played so great and grand a part in Grecian tragedy ; when the prophetic writers of the Bible are read in a natural sense it cannot fail to be seen what a stress they laid upon "the confidence of a good descent." It was a proverb in Israel, " The fathers have eaten sour grapes and the children's teeth are set on edge." Here, then, and in this relation, may be noted the instructive fact that just as moral feeling was the first function to be affected at the beginning of mental derangement in the individual, so now the defect or absence of it is seen to mark the way of degeneracy through generations.

It was the latest acquisition of mental evolution ; it is the first to go in mental dissolution.

A second fact of observation may be set down as worthy of observation, if not of immediate acceptation, namely, that an absence of moral feeling in one generation, as shown by a mean, selfish, and persistent disregard of moral action in the conduct of life, may be the cause of mental derangement in the next generation. In fact, a person may succeed in producing insanity in his progeny by a persistent disuse of moral feeling, and a continuous exercise throughont his life of those selfish, mean, and anti-social tendencies which are a negation of the highest moral relations of mankind. He does not ever exercise the nervous substrata which minister to moral functions, wherefore they undergo atrophy in him, and he runs the risk of transmitting them to his progeny in so imperfect a state that they are incapable of full development in them ; just as the instinct of an animal which is not exercised for many generations, on account of changed conditions of life, becomes less distinct by degrees, and, in the end, perhaps, extinct. In sober truth the lessons of morality which were proclaimed by the prophets of old as indispensable to the stability and well being of families and nations, were not mere visions of vague fancy ; founded upon actual observation and intuition of the laws of nature working in human events they were insights into the eternal truths of human evolution.*

Whether, then, man goes upwards or downwards, undergoes development or degeneration, we have equally to do with matters of stern law. Provision has been made for both ways ; it has been left to him to find out and to determine which way he shall take. And it is plain that he must find the right path of evolution, and avoid the wrong path of degeneracy, by observation and experience, pursuing the same method of positive inquiry which has served him so well in the different sciences.

Being preëminently and essentially a social being,

---

* The most ancient books of the Parsees, the Zend-Avesta, proclaim, under the form of a myth, the operation of the law of heredity, in respect to the moral nature ; (Zend-Avesta, Vol. iii., pp. 351–378) ; the book of Mosaïsm, the Bible, reproduces this myth in its first pages, from whence the legends and traditions of Islamism have been borrowed ; (*Aperçu historique sur le temps anté-islamiques. Revue indépendante.* PERRON, directeur de l'école de Médecine du Caire, Vol. V., pp. 445–450) ; the evangelists put, two several times, into the mouth of Christ, the knowledge of the principle which he revives, first, in the discourse on judgment, and in a parable ; (Matthew, chap. xii., verse 33) ; secondly, in the most daring reproach directed against the Pharasees (Matthew, chap. xxiii., verses 29–34).

each one the member of one body—the unit, that is, in the social organism—the laws which he has to observe and obey are not the physical laws of nature only, but also those higher laws which govern the relations of individuals in the social state. If he makes his observations sincerely and adequately in this way he cannot fail to perceive that the laws of morality were not really miraculous revelations from heaven, any more than was the discovery of the law of gravitation, but that they were essential conditions of social evolution, and were learned practically by the stern lessons of experience. He has learned his duty to his neighbor as he has learned his duty to nature; it is implicit in the complex society of men dwelling together in peace and unity, and it has been revealed explicitly by the intuition of a few extraordinary men of sublime moral genius.*

As it is not a true, it cannot be a useful, notion to foster that morality was the special gift to man, and is the special property of any theological system, and that its life is bound up essentially with the life of any such creed. It is not religious creed which has invented and been the basis of morality, but morality which has been the bulwark of religions. And as a

---

* A considerable amount of mischief is done by the complacent vanity with which man demonstrates his superior relations to other animals, in place of laboring earnestly to develop those relations to something higher which undoubtedly exists potentially in him ; for the progression which has been observed in nature should rightly be realized in the events of human life—in the history of mankind as well as in the history of the individual. Were it not that all men are only too glad to pull down the mighty to their level, "to pare the mountain to the plain" one might wonder that no one has tried to prove these men of genius of a different species from the common ruck of mortals—" Οὐκ δἶσθα ὅτι ἡμίθεοι ὶ ἥρωες," as Socrates says (Cratylus, ch. xxxii.). They only struggled upwards with success as it is the beneficent purpose of nature that all should do.

matter of fact, it is certain that morality has suffered many times, not a little from its connection with theological creeds ; that its truths have been appropriated and used to support demoralizing superstitions which were no part of it ; that doctrines essentially immoral have been even taught in the name of religion ; and that religious systems, in their struggles to establish their supremacy, have oftentimes shown small respect to the claims of morality.*

Had religion been true to its nature and function, as wide as morality and humanity, it should have been the bond of unity to hold mankind together in one brotherhood, linking them in good feeling, good will, and good work toward one another.

If we would learn to reason closely, we must learn to be good doubters. Doubt, determined doubt, is the only key which unlocks the caskets of certain knowledge. We have so many lame philosophies because we have so few thorough doubters. It is not the spirit of doubt, as bishops and parsons sing, which hinders the progress of truth and religion ; but the spirit of assumption. Why have we all these disgraceful divisions, wranglings, and heart-burnings in science and theology ? It is not because men will doubt too much, but because they will not doubt enough. It is because they hate the trouble of doubting in themselves, and resent its reasonable demands in others, that we are flooded with sham philosophies, superstitions and infidelities.

Fortunate is it, then, for the interests of morality that it is not bound up essentially with any form of

*See "History of the Inquisition of the Middle Ages." Henry C. Lea, New York, 1887.
"History of European Morals." W. E. H. Lecky, New York, 1869.

religious creed, but that it survives when creeds die,
having its more secure foundations in the hard won
experience of mankind.

The inquiry which, taking a sincere survey of the
facts, finds the basis and sanction of morality in experience, by no means arrives in the end at easy lessons of self-indulgence for the individual and the race,
but on the contrary at the hardest lessons of self-
renunciation. Disclosing to man the stern and uniform
reign of law in nature, even in the evolution and degeneracy of his own nature, it takes from him the
comfortable but demoralizing doctrine that he or
others can escape the penalty of his ignorance, error,
or wrong doings, either by penitence or prayer, and
holds him to the strictest account for them. Discard-
ing the notion that the observed uniformity of nature
is but a uniformity of sequence at will, which may be
interrupted whenever its interruption is earnestly enough
asked for, a notion which were it more than lip doctrine must necessarily deprive him of his most urgent
motive to study patiently the laws of nature in order
to conform to them, it enforces a stern feeling of responsibility to search out painfully the right path of
obedience and to follow it, inexorably laying upon man
the responsibility of the future of his race.

If it be most certain, as it is, that all disobedience
of natural law, whether physical or moral, is avenged
inexorably in its consequences on earth, either upon the
individual himself, or more often, perhaps, upon others,
that the violated law cannot be bribed to stay its arm
by burnt offerings, nor placated by prayers, it is a harm-
ful doctrine as tending directly to undermine understanding and to weaken will, to teach that either prayer

or sacrifice will obviate the consequences of want of
foresight or want of self-discipline, or that reliance upon
supernatural aid will make amends for lack of intelligent will. We read and we do well to read regularly
the ten commandments, and we still pray half heartedly
in our churches—as our forefathers prayed with their
whole hearts—that our hearts may be inclined to keep
them. Yet is there a person of sincere understanding
who, uttering that prayer, does not know well that, if
it is to be answered, he must cleanse his hands, purify
his heart, and put in force, in his moral world, those
other sanitary measures which experience has proved to
be efficacious, and that the aid vouchsafed to the
prayer will only be given when these are by themselves
succesful? To get rid of the notion of supernatural intervention is the essential condition of true knowledge
and self-help in this matter.

If the matter be made one simply of scientific observation it must be confessed that all the evidence goes
to prove that the events of the moral world are matters of law and order equally with those of the physical
world, and that supernatural interpositions have no more
place in the one than in the other ; that he who prays
for the creation of a clean heart and the renewal of a
right spirit within him, if he gets at last what he prays
for, gets it by the operation of the ordinary laws of
moral growth and development, in consequence of pains-
taking watchfulness over himself, and the continual exercise of good resolves. Only when he gets it in that
way will he get the benefit of supernatural aid ; and if
he rests in the belief of supernatural aid, without taking
pains to get it entirely in that way, he will do himself
moral harm ; for if he cannot rely upon special inter-

positions in the moral any more than in the physical world, if he has to do entirely with those secondary laws of nature, through which alone the supernatural is made natural, the invisible visible, it needs no demonstration that the opposite belief cannot strengthen but must weaken the understanding and the will. It is plain that true moral hygiene is as impossible to him who relies upon supernatural power to change his heart, to the neglect of the proper means provided, as sanitary science is impossible to the savage who relies upon his fetich to stay a pestilence or plague and neglects to clean away dirt.*

When it is properly understood, natural science sets before man a higher intellectual aim than he is ever likely to reach by metaphysical paths and raises a more self-sacrificing moral standard.

---

* When a great and sudden revolution in the *Ego* is produced by an external cause it is full of hazard to the mental stability of the individual, and very apt to become pathological ; nothing is more perilous to the equilibrium of a character than for anyone to be placed in entirely changed external circumstances without his inner life having been gradually adapted thereto ; and madness, when its origin is fairly examined, always means discord between the individual and his circumstances. Dr. Channing, in a sermon *On the Evil of Sin*, speaking of the absurdity of the notion that in changing worlds there will be a change of character, says : ——— "In the first place, it contradicts all our experience of the nature and the laws of the mind. There is nothing more striking in the mind than the connection of its successive states. Our present knowledge, thoughts, feelings, and characters, are the result of former impressions, passions, and pursuits. We are in this moment what the past made us ; and to suppose that, at death, the influences of our whole past course are to cease on our minds, and that a character is to spring up altogether at war with what has preceded it, is to suppose the most important law or principle of the mind to be violated, is to destroy all analogy between the present and future, and to substitute for experience the wildest dreams of fancy. In truth, such a sudden revolution in the character, as is here supposed, seems to destroy man's identity. The individual thus transformed can hardly seem to himself or to others the same being. It is equivalent to the creation of a new soul."—"The Works of William E. Channing, D.D." Vol. IV, p. 159. Boston, 1848.

For when all has been said, it is not the most elevated or the most healthy business for a man to be occupied continually with anxieties and apprehensions and cares about the salvation of his own soul, and to be earnest to do well in this life in order that he may escape eternal suffering, and gain eternal happiness, in the life to come. An altruistic end, as the prime motive of well doing, is the strongest and noblest motive to well doing ; with the incarnation of Divine Wisdom, we are taught, there was an annihilation of self. Can anyone hesitate to declare that it is better for a man's self, and best for his kind to have fought with the beasts of unrighteousness even if the dead rise not? To make his life subserve the good of his kind, to promote the well being of the social organization of which he is a unit, is the plain and inevitable conclusion which science enforces as to his true function and highest development.

The golden rule of morals was perceived and proclaimed long before it received its highest Christian expression.* Modern science teaches no new morality. It simply brings men back to that which has been the central lesson and real stay of the great religions of the world, and which is implicit in the constitution of society, and it does this in a way that promises to bring the

---

* There appears to be no doubt that Confucius, among others, had the clearest apprehension of it and expressly taught it ; and the Buddhist religion of perfection is certainly founded upon self-conquest and self-sacrifice. They are its very corner-stone; the purification of the mind from unholy desires and passions, and a devotion to the good of others, which rises to an enthusiasm for humanity in order to escape the miseries of this life and to attain to a perfect moral repose. " Let all the sins that have been committed fall upon me, in order that the world may be delivered," Buddha says. And of the son or disciple of Buddha it is said : " When reviled he revileth not again ; when smitten he bears the blow without resentment; when treated with anger and passion he returns love and good will ; when threatened with death he bears no malice."

understanding into entire harmony with the will, and to
promote by a close and consistent interaction their ac-
cordant growth and development ; it strips morality of
the livery of superstition, in which theological creeds
have dressed it, and presents it to the adoration of
mankind in its natural purity and strength. Mighty, it
must be allowed, is the power of the human will ; that
which, to him whose will is not developed, is *fate*, is to
him who has a well-fashioned will *power ;* so much has
been conquered from necessity, so much has been taken
from the devil's territory.

The scientific spirit of the age preaches self-renunciation. The investigations of Geology, revealing the existence of the earth for thousands of years before man
appeared upon it,—the discoveries of Astronomy, showing how small a fragment the earth is in the vast im-
mensity of the universe,—the records of history teach-
ing the littleness of man in the mighty course of nature,
—and the researches of the chemist and physiologist
proving the very close relationship of man to the flower
which he tramples upon and the dust which he despises,
—all tend to dispel human blindness and to humble
human arrogance. How persistently has the self-hood
of mankind opposed these revelations of his humble position in the universe ! Willingly or unwillingly, however, man must indeed acknowledge them—nay, must
indeed believe it possible that the sun may rise when
there is no human eye to behold it, that the birds may
sing when there is no human ear to listen, that the flowers may bloom and the fruits may ripen when there is no
human hand to pluck them, that the course of nature
may continue though all men have perished. For it is a
supposition which the history of the past does not re-

ject, that, after man has disappeared from the earth, other and higher beings may take his place and rejoice in the beauties of nature as he has rejoiced in them.

If the lesson of self-renunciation is distinctly taught to humanity, with how much greater force is it taught to the individual mortal. It is a natural vanity in every-one to think that he will be greatly missed when life's fitful dream is ended; and yet how little is the loss of the most distinguished felt. When he is gone to his everlasting rest it seems that he has rightly gone, and his place is so filled up that he seems no longer wanted. A little while and who thinks of "the touch of a vanished hand"?—who remembers "the sound of the voice that is still?" Life refuses to carry with it the dead body of grief; for death is the condition of new life. The storied urn last only for a few gen-erations at most, but the living work which a man has done never dies; it is a monument which outlasts time, which the universe cannot destroy unless it destroys itself.

As far as we can judge, the force in the universe is a constant quantity. Nothing appears to be added and nothing is taken away. When the force of man is aug-mented in mental development, it is evidently at the expense of nature; and when man degenerates, nature increases at his expense. The correlation which is be-lieved to exist between the physical forces may be sup-posed to exist between them and the mental or vital force. Speculation on the matter is, however, of no avail, and must always come back to the same place where it has been times and times before.

If we ask whence comes this impulse, we can only answer tamely that it comes from the same unfathomable source as the impulse which inspires or moves organic evolution throughout nature. He who reflects upon himself and the universe is forced in the end to the recognition in the workings of the world of a power from which all life and energy proceed, which has been from the beginning, is now, and, so far as we can see, ever shall be, and which cannot be comprehended or controlled by human thought or will, but comprehends and controls human thought and will. We recognize an impulsion outside ourselves, working also in our wills, which is the moving energy of the evolution which went on through countless ages before man appeared, which is going on now in his progress, and which will doubtless go on through countless ages after he has ceased to replenish the earth and subdue it. We come back, indeed, to something which, however we may name it or forbear to name it, is very like the theological Trinity—the Unrevealed and Unrevealable, the Revealed and the Revealer. In human thought and will, nature has arrived at self-consciousness, but the power which impels the highest evolution of life as manifested in the highest reach of human thought and will is fundamentally the same power which impels the evolution of the lowest forms of life.

The nature of the Deity as the creator and governor of the world is not within the scope of scientific investigation. A scientific investigation of the nature of the Deity by the method of observation and induction is for obvious reasons impossible. Mental science does not seek to fathom the abysses of the Infinite. It does not attempt to explain the being and the nature of God, nor the origin of evil, nor to give any reason for the existence of the universe. In its survey of facts it simply views mental development, whether in the individual or in the race, as a process of organization as the consummate display of nature's organic evolution, and recognizes the most favorable conditions of such evolution to be the most intimate harmony between man and nature. It also teaches him lessons of reverence and humility, for it teaches him in the first place not to despise and call unclean the supreme product of evolution, the last and best work of his Creator's hand ; and secondly, not impiously to circumscribe supernatural power by the narrow limits of his understanding, but to bethink himself that it were just as easy in the beginning, or now, or at any time, for the Almighty Creator of matter and its properties to make it think as to make mind think.

We can say no more now than what Empedocles said in the 'Olympiads,' " All things are but a mingling and a separation of the mingled, which are called life and death by ignorant mortals;" however closely we trace the order of events the mystery of the *why* remains where it was ; the power which determines why one tissue supervenes on another, why life should tend upwards, which inspires and guides the everlasting becoming of things, must ever remain past finding out.

Meanwhile the abortive lines which vice produces, and the great miseries which are witnessed, are examples excellently well adapted for the formation of correct inductions in the spirit of positive science ; they are pathological instances—experiments supplied by nature— tending to the correction of unjust theories, and the establishment of true generalizations. Far, then, from being useless, they are beneficial, as they are inevitable, in the purpose of nature ; with mankind generally, as with man individually, it is out of suffering that knowledge comes. If each age would but believe that the whole universe had not been created solely for its satisfaction, and if each individual in the age would but learn that he is a very insignificant atom in the great whole, then, perhaps, it might be possible to look with less impatience, and more calmness, on those events which are painful, and do not accord with the human ideal of what should be.

Sufficient is it for each one to feel that with the definite aim of the development of his moral and intellectual nature before him, he must work definitely for that object, must pursue with quiet constancy his course, "like a star without haste, yet without rest," in other matters, outside his orbit, and beyond the reach of his faculties, being content to "stretch lame hands of faith," and "faintly trust the larger hope."

The belief in the supernatural is often an honest and avowed belief entertained by many great men; it is, however, one in which we cannot for a moment concur. To us supernaturalism is an absurdity; if it exists, it exists not for us, as color exists not for the blind, nor sound for the deaf. We believe in only one supernatural existence, namely, in the omnipotent Creator of matter and its properties—the power which made nature —the father and friend of man. We believe in the book of Nature and its author; in the world and in God. But as for the supernatural, the spirit world of sights and sounds, the whole tribe of apparitions, the whole chime of ghostly voices, the delusive phenomena of the "spiritists," the zoists, the mesmerists, the mystics, the credulous enthusiasts, *et hoc omne genus,* we believe that they can, one and all of them, be explained upon the principles of physical or meta-physical law. A large number of them are pure and simple fictions; others, intended only at first as an expression of imaginative thought, have been mistaken for realities; others again have been, neither more nor less, the expressions of partial insanity. It is certainly not to be denied that a belief in a supernatural intervention in human affairs might be useful at one stage of human evolution, and indeed essential to social progress, just as it is essential to a child's welfare to believe in and respect its own parents, who may nevertheless be unworthy of respect, and yet may be mischievous at a later stage when it has done its work and undergoes decay; the intellect having outgrown it. It is a sad mission to cut through and destroy with the scissors of analysis the delicate and iridescent veil with which our proud mediocrity envelops itself. It may be a sad thing to strike away that crutch which alone seems to support the feebleness of humanity, but it is plain that for a man to lean habitually and heavily on a crutch is not the way to learn to walk firmly; he will do that best by risking many falls and by making more skillful trials after each fall; and in like manner he who has to learn and to do in a world of natural law will find his true good in getting strength through suffering, skill through trial, victory through obedience, and not in reliance on supernatural interpositions, which have hitherto occurred for the most part where there was no need for their occurrence, and have failed to occur where they were most wanted—where their help would have been not superfluous, but serviceable.

When Christians assemble together in holy communion, to break bread in memory of the life and sufferings of the Saviour, they solemnly renew and attest

their conviction of the essentiality to human welfare of
the sublime moral truths which he proclaimed in speech,
realized in his life, and suffered for in his death, and
quicken their sense of them, which is apt to grow dull
in the rude conflicts of the world. We get strength
and comfort to go on the narrow way of uprightness,
from this assembling of ourselves together in solemn
meeting, out of our consent of faith and the infection
of sympathy ; for we are beings of the same kind, struggling with the same trials, bearing the same sorrows, and
looking forward to the same end of our labors under the
sun. But it cannot, therefore, be argued that there is
anything which does not come by ordinary mental laws,
anything supernatural, in the moral enthusiasm which
is kindled in these circumstances.

If a number of persons were gathered together in
the same sympathetic way to fan some unwise, emotional excitement and to do some foolish thing, the excitement would be augmented, and the infection of it
would spread by sympathy in the same way. The infection of emotion has, as history shows, given rise to
many moral epidemics.

If it come to pass that man is robbed of that in-
tensely personal feeling which is poured out in appre-
hensive wails about the salvation of his own soul, or in
emotional strains by writers of the spasmodic and fleshly
school of poetry, or in morbidly subtle analysis of over-
strained feelings of any sort, there will be no harm
done ; for it is a sort of emotion that is as unwholesome
as a hysterical ecstacy. Let him attain instead to that
calmer, deeper, wider, and healthier emotion which is
subordinated to pure insight into the harmonies of
nature, and to philosophical survey of its serene order

and is applied objectively to give warmth of tone and
color to their expression in words.   The creed of nature
is not shrieking self-assertion, but serene self-surrender ;
not man against the universe, but man as a part of
the universe ; not individual life with the single aim of
securing a blissful immortality, but individual life in
subordination to the general life.

Assuredly the "everlasting arms" are beneath the
upright man who dealeth uprightly, but they are the
everlasting laws of nature which sustain him who, doing
that which is lawful and right, leads a life that is in
faithful harmony with Nature's progress.   The destruction which falls upon him who dealeth treacherously
and doeth iniquity, "observing not the Commandments
of the Lord to obey them" are the avenging consequences of broken natural laws.

I do not know how far the student of theology
may be, or think himself to be, free to study a science,
which like all natural science, whatever must certainly
lead to a remodelling of all creeds ; and I shall not
venture to express an opinion on that point.   But I
feel myself quite free to say that mental science
will assuredly afford a solid support to all the great
doctrines of Christianity whether they be of faith
or morals, whenever the intelligent theologian seeks
its aid.   The sermon which scientific psychology
preaches to-day is the sermon which nearly nineteen
hundred years ago was preached from the Mount of
Olives near Jerusalem.   I can speak with less scruple
as to the student of law.   To him mental science will
offer the means of determining the true nature of evidence ; the origin of beliefs and convictions ; the just
extent of responsibility—personal, parental, social ; the

uses and abuses of punishment; and the best means of
reformation of criminals and classes of criminals.

      It must be confessed that those who pursue the
study of the physical sciences do appear, in their enthusiasm for their special work, sometimes to lose sight of
that which is the end of all science, and to propound as
sufficient for human instruction, guidance, and conduct
that which is practically a negation of anything like a
doctrine adequate to embrace the phenomena of human
feeling and conduct.   Men will have some faith to live
by.   Revolutions in human conduct do not appear to
have come from the intellect in times past; again and
again that which seemed the foolishness of the simple
has confounded the wisdom of the wise; and it is not
impossible that when the students of physical science
have made it all so plain that a wayfaring man, though
a fool, cannot go wrong, if he will only keep his eyes
open, some untaught person "out of Galilee," a friend
of publicans and sinners, who happens to be inspired
with strong moral sympathies, will stir up a wave of
feeling which shall sweep over the paths, and hardly
leave a trace of them behind.

     "Bless not thyself only," says the author of the
Religio Medici, "that thou wert born at Athens; but
among thy multiplied acknowledgments lift up one hand
to heaven that thou wert born of honest parents, that
modesty, humility, patience, and veracity lay in the same
egg, and came into the world with thee.   From such
foundations thou mayest be happy in a virtuous pre-
cocity, and make an early and long walk in goodness;
so mayest thou feel the contrary vice unto nature, and
resist some by the antidote of thy temper."   Schiller has
somewhere said: "This is the peculiar curse of evil, that

it must continually reproduce evil;" and one may confidently add : This is the peculiar blessing of good, that it must continually reproduce good.

If the science of Psychology is to prove of good service in the cause of civilization,—if it be destined to add to the blessings of social life, to promote and diffuse well doing and happiness throughout society, and further the great and noble cause of truth and Christian charity among men, then will the question now raised come in for a large share of the attention of the really wise and good, of those—

> " Whose actions teach
> More virtue than a sect can preach ; "

and not the less of those who

> " Hold that ever
> Virtue and knowledge are endowments greater "

than nobleness and riches.

www.ingramcontent.com/pod-product-compliance
Lightning Source LLC
Chambersburg PA
CBHW021427090426
42742CB00009B/1285